VOICE OF EMPIRE
A Centennial Sketch of *The Denver Post*

By William H. Hornby

D0732709

Colorado Historical Society   1992

Printed in the United States of America

Library of Congress Cataloging-in-Publication Data

Hornby, William H. (William Harry), 1923-
    Voice of empire : a centennial sketch of The Denver post / by
William H. Hornby.
        p. cm.
    Includes index.
    ISBN 0-942576-32-2
    1. Denver post—History—20th century. 2. Denver (Colo.)—Social
conditions—20th century. I. Title.
PN4899.D45P618   1992
071.8883—dc20
                                                    92-2236
                                                    CIP

Contents

Throughout 1991, as The Denver Post *approached its centennial year, these sketches appeared in the author's regular column. The series, an unusual investment of space for a newspaper, would not have been possible without the much-appreciated understanding and support of the* Post's *editorial page editor, Chuck Green, and of publisher Donald F. Hunt. Research and production assistance for the series has been gratefully received from longtime* Post *staffers Isabelle Holmes, Joyce Anderson and Ray Dangel.*

Denver Post *headlines, various years.*

Front page, July 21, 1969

Prologue

■ _____

The Denver Post turned 100 years on August 8, 1992. Allowing for mechanical breakdowns, publishing disruptions, and human error, all of which sometimes happen in the news trade, that amounts to approximately 35,000 editions that have been plunked into the daily lives of hundreds of thousands of readers. That is a lot of information for this Western American region and for its metropolitan capital's population, which under the *Post*'s gaze has grown from a young 100,000 to a young 1,600,000. Talk about mountains, which are Denver's traditional topic! All those *Denver Posts* would make a mountain of news, of ads, of entertainment, of causes, political fights, paper, ink, expense, energy, creativity, and not a little heartache. And, for that matter, it would make a mountain of hundreds of people in all the halls of Mother *Post*'s fascinating, creative mansion—owners, editors, reporters, photographers, ad salesmen, business managers, accountants, printers, layout staff, mailers, artists, ad creators, circulators, lawyers, bankers, computerizers, shills, saints, phone operators, office managers, and the secretaries who really run things. How many, many of them have lived the *Post* story only to go on like yesterday's news! They all were—and are—chords in the "Voice of the Rocky Mountain Empire," a label that symbolizes the *Post*'s century-long climb to national recognition as the significant editorial voice of the Mountain West, just as Denver has become the Mountain West's significant city-civilization.

That both the *Post* and Denver got there together is not an accident but the result of a city-building process that few journalists or historians appreciate. Sometimes, like Denver's, the *Post*'s early climb was gaudy and greedy, raucous and vulgar. Over the years, this newspaper has been hated as much as loved, scorned as much as envied, during its 100 years of reaching for the heights and of sometimes falling to the depths. Like the city whose history it mirrors, the newspaper has tread water in bad financial times as well as floating serenely in the good.

Talking about bad times, it is ironical to those who discover patterns in history that the *Post* entered its first century from the ruins of Denver's first great financial collapse, the silver bust of 1893, and faces its second from the equally chaotic energy and real estate wreckage of the late 1980s. But always surviving ruthless business competition, the *Post* has been helping its city-state compete to overcome both geographic isolation and population explosion.

Western American newspapers, historian Daniel Boorstin records, were different from their European and Atlantic Coast forerunners. In *The Americans: The National Experience,* he writes of the booster press in the "upstart" cities that developed in the West: "In Europe, newspapers had arisen to serve the needs, at first of a small literary or literate circle, later of a larger reading community. Similarly, the early newspapers on the Atlantic seaboard, often begun by an official 'Publick Printer,' were produced to satisfy the interests of people already there. . . . But the pioneer newspaper of the upstart city, like the Western railroad, had to call into being the very population it aimed to serve." This work of Western newspapers in creating the communities they hoped to serve yielded characteristics which make the American newspaper different from those elsewhere. Boorstin suggests that the great spread in numbers and varieties of papers in America, and the zeal with which they guard their freedom from government or political control, stem from this pioneering march of American journalism into the journalistically empty, community-building West.

This westward movement of newspaper journalism, according to Boorstin, also gave our newspapers a distinctively "community-centered and non-ideological emphasis." From the beginning, he states, "large numbers of American newspapers were the advance advertising agents of new communities. If they were subsidized, it was, with few exceptions, by local businessmen interested in community building, rather than by ideologues with an axe to grind. . . . Some American newspapermen have called this preoccupation with the local community the leading characteristic, the principal novelty, and the secret strength of American journalism."

Anyone with a working knowledge of Denver's history will recognize the truth of Boorstin's analysis, particularly as they consider the history of Denver and *The Denver Post*. Readers may want to consider, for the overall city, Stephen J. Leonard and Thomas J. Noel's history of Denver, *Denver: Mining Camp to Metropolis;* for the *Post*, Gene Fowler's colorful *Timber Line* and Bill Hosokawa's accurate *Thunder in the Rockies;* and for the *News*, Robert Perkin's *The First Hundred Years*. But most of these sources are outdated and do not take into consideration modern changes in the communications scene, such as the advent of television and the single-parent family. And they emphasize the jazzy personalities and episodes of newspaper history at the expense of perceiving the newspaper as a city-builder and as a regional voice on the national scene.

The Denver Post's history roughly breaks into these periods: From 1892 to 1895, it was a tiny, weak political sheet of several owners and no great distinction. From 1895 to 1980 it was the dominant local paper owned by the Bonfils and Tammen families. And that local ownership era is roughly divided in half by World War II (1939–45), before which the paper was a sensational, isolationist, and occasionally bigoted journal, and after which it became nationally recognized as an ethical, internationalist regional daily. From 1980 to 1990, the national group ownership of Times Mirror Corporation and, now, of MediaNews Group, have modernized the paper and saved it from financial collapse in the barracudinal economy of the 1980s. All of these ownerships and the people who worked for them have loved the paper and seen that it survived to become the "Voice of the Rocky Mountain Empire."

Harry H. Tammen and Frederick G. Bonfils, ca. 1895, reproduced from the twenty-five-year jubilee edition of The Denver Post, *1917.*

THE CIRCUS YEARS
The Era of Bonfils and Tammen

I

Few physical traces are left to remind us of Denver when *The Denver Post* was born. By 1892 the frontier hamlet founded just thirty–three years before had become the nation's twenty-sixth largest city, second behind San Francisco in the West, with 106,000 people. It had electric lighting, telephones, and street-cars. But cows still grazed in vacant lots among the new mansions on Capitol Hill, and horse manure and outhouses abounded. On the streets, mostly unpaved, horse and buggy jousted with tram, bike, and pedestrian; the blessings of car and airplane were decades ahead. Stephen J. Leonard and Thomas J. Noel, in *Denver: Mining Camp to Metropolis*, set the scene:

> From Capitol Hill, visitors to Denver in the 1890s could survey the sprawling young city. Two dozen streetcar lines shot from downtown out to suburbs bristling with tree saplings. To the north, sulfurous smoke belched from Globeville smelter chimneys, the most prominent features on the skyline. . . . In the winter, coal smoke ruined the view and fouled the air. Worse still were the smells of overcrowded neighborhoods such as the densely packed Chinese section at Six-teenth and Wazee. . . . Wags joked, "There are more flies in Denver than anywhere else in the world and they stick more."
>
> What casual observers did not see was a city overwhelmed by growth; a place largely peopled by former farmers, ex-miners, small-town and rural folk. . . . Few were born in Denver, most had lived in the city only a few years, and many were rootless transients ready to

move on. . . . Most . . . were firm in their belief that social progress was best promoted by unrestrained competition. The fit, they believed, would survive and prosper.

For those who were thus "fit," the 1880s had been mostly boom-boom. Ever-growing railroad strength had enlarged Denver's commercial and distribution grasp on the mountain mining industry. One hundred million dollars from the silver mines, and the colorful humans who had made it, descended to the comforts of the Queen City, many such as H. A. W. Tabor and Charles Boettcher coming from the "Cloud City" of Leadville on the Continental Divide. The few lived well in mansions and business buildings as fine as anything back East; the many struggled in shops and smelters and lived in more modest homes such as those now recalled by the Ninth Street Historic Park on the Auraria campus in downtown Denver. One can sense some of the 1890s downtown business ambience from such preserved historic buildings as the Brown Palace Hotel; the Equitable, Masonic, Kittredge, and Boston buildings; the Denver Dry Goods Company; and Trinity Methodist and Central Presbyterian churches. These stone buildings remind us that the growing commercial population was pressing "uptown" from the old center around Union Station, Lower Downtown, and Larimer Street.

With many of the Capitol Hill mansions and the older public schools, Richard Brettell in *Historic Denver* believes that this 1888–93 building boom gave Denver its "most expansive, inventive, and experimental architecture"—the kind of city the "fit" people of Denver, themselves just a few years away from the shanty and the saloon, were building. It was not too hard to forget on Capitol Hill that "other" Denver of tents, shacks, and huts along Cherry Creek and the South Platte River, of coal smoke, stockyard stench, and smelter fumes, of three hundred saloons and a thousand whores. Overall, the thrust of Denver leaders in the 1880s and 1890s was what Noel calls a "rush to respectability."

But Denver was heading for an economic bust that wiped out some of the respectability for the thirty-one millionaires the city had acquired. The Colorado economy was squeamish as over the nation and region vital railroads faced bankruptcy. The range cattle industry was suffering from overgrazing and the hangover from the disastrous winter of 1887. On the Colorado plains sodbusters were moving in, falsely thinking that the heavy rains of the 1880s would grace the 1890s. Politically, the People's party, known as the Populists, was attacking the railroads, the corporations, the mining stock speculations, the unfair treatment of farmers, the vested interests of the major parties, and playing to the growing frustrations of subsistence farmers and wage earners. Colorado even elected a Populist governor in 1892.

On top of it all came the collapse of silver prices. Colorado was mining 60 percent of the nation's silver, most of it sold to the government for coinage. When the Democratic administration of Grover Cleveland decided to reduce buying, the Colorado mining industry was dealt a blow from which it never fully recovered. Prices collapsed, mines shut down, unemployed miners fled to Denver, twelve banks failed in mid-1893, building starts dropped from 2,000 a year to 200, real estate balloons in the streetcar suburbs punctured, and many barons like Horace Tabor were ruined, Baby Doe or no Baby Doe.

In this hectic economic climate, reminiscent of our own day, *The Denver Post* was spawned of the political partisanship that drove most newspaper ownerships in those days. The non-electronic media of the young city then included five daily newspapers, thirty-seven weeklies, and twenty-two monthly publications. The three well-established dailies were all connected to political parties or business interest groups: the *Rocky Mountain News*, staunchly Democratic, owned by Senator Thomas Patterson; the *Denver Republican* by smelter king Nathaniel Hill; and the *Denver Times* by banker David H. Moffat and his circle. When Patterson and the *News* temporarily deserted the regular Democratic party and President Cleveland over the silver issue, a group of loyalists put up $50,000 and started the *Post*. But the harsh economic competition and the unpopularity of the official, anti–free silver Democratic party suspended the paper in little more than a year. It was restored for another $100,000 and renamed the *Evening Post* on June 22, 1894, still as a Democratic organ, but politics and skimpy business again emptied the till, and by late 1895 the paper sold again in a "fire-sale" for $12,500.

The buyers were Harry H. Tammen, thirty-nine, and Frederick G. Bonfils, thirty-four. Tammen, a curio shop owner and ex-bartender, and Bonfils, a Kansas lottery operator, seemed of doubtful credentials to the owners of the other Denver dailies. They smacked of the more disreputable frontier that the mansion-moguls were trying to forget. But they put out their first issue on October 28, 1895, and in a very few years, with a brand of flamboyant circus journalism that was shrewdly targeted at the economically shaken and mostly rootless mass of new Denverites, *The Denver Post* built more circulation than the others combined. The next time the newspaper was sold, eighty-five years later, the going price was $95 million!

II

One of the grey-bearded arguments in this business is whether editors and writers or the owners and publishers make the greater contribution to a newspaper's fundamental character. It is painful for a career editor to confess, but the 100-year history of *The Denver Post* suggests that ownerships should be the prime targets for newspaper historians. For skillful and colorful editors and writers come and go, but the ownerships hire them, outfit them and blaze their trail, and fire or bury them when their time has come. And the owners make the fundamentally good or bad guesses that grant or deny a newspaper's economic survival.

As with most other major American newspapers, *The Denver Post* has enjoyed several ownerships that have thus defined its character in different ways. As previously sketched, those from 1892 to 1895 were a group of politicians who flew in the face of community business sentiment by hawking the unpopular anti-silver policies of the national Democratic administration. As heir to their economic bad guesses came the eighty-five-year regime of the Bonfils-Tammen families, who turned the *Post* into a politically independent, populist, highly flamboyant journal, a formula that proved to be a very good economic guess. After World War II the heirs of Bonfils and Tammen, in what amounted in practice if not on the record to a distinctly different ownership, turned the *Post* into a much less flamboyant newspaper with a growing national reputation but of equally growing costs and shrinking dividends—an uncertain economic guess. From 1981 on, the Times Mirror Corporation and MediaNews group owners, facing severe economic recession and the fierce competition of television and nationally distributed dailies, modernized to meet new reading habits and production technologies, while retaining the Western and Denver editorial leadership built over the years.

When Frederick G. Bonfils and Harry H. Tammen, both in their thirties, bought the *Post* in 1895, they seemed to the rest of the Denver newspaper fraternity an inexperienced and—to Denver society—highly suspect pair. Tammen was known as a former bartender at the Windsor Hotel, the owner of a prosperous curio business which exported ersatz Western artifacts such as fake Indian scalps, and publisher from 1889 to 1896 of *The Great Divide*, a monthly magazine of Western regional (and curio) promotion.

Early students of the *Post* have made light of this previous publishing experience, but more recent research by Mort Stern of Georgetown, Colorado, suggests that *The Great Divide* brought Tammen into contact with such well-known journalism personalities of the time as Joseph Medill of the *Chicago Tribune* and J. Walter Thompson, the New York founder of the modern advertising industry. The famous Eastern editor and future author William Dean Howells considered Tammen's magazine "one of the most interesting of American monthlies," and at its peak it had a respectable circulation of about 50,000. Certainly through this magazine, Tammen learned about the populist tastes of a growing mass reading public that was then unentertained by any broadcast sirens. He also sensed the topical attractiveness of "The West" and its denizens.

If Tammen was the puckish curio huckster and born promoter of Gene Fowler's 1933 *Timber Line,* he was also a man

9

seriously interested in publishing about the West. Stern writes that *The Great Divide* not only offered "romances and adventures as well as history of cowboys, ranchers, miners, and their women, but there were serious articles about other regions of the nation and the world, about technological advance, about prehistoric and current Indians, about animals, birds, flowers and minerals—as well as gemstones and similar collectibles that Tammen, the proprietor, would sell or offer as premiums." In short, Tammen recognized that the general populace was hungry for some entertainment in the fare pouring from the new generation of presses.

The Great Divide moved to Chicago, and Tammen took considerable economic blows in the silver crash of 1893. By 1895, when the *Post* came up for sale, the ever-cheerful, self-made son of German immigrants had a yearning to buy, but not the dollars. How he found his financing and a lifetime trusted partner in Bonfils, a Kansas City lottery operator and land speculator, has several versions in *Denver Post* lore; however, the most respected *Post* historian, Bill Hosokawa, accepts the story that the two met in Chicago when Tammen, hawking reprints of the Declaration of Independence, ran across at the printer's some lottery tickets destined for Bonfils. Sensing a prospect, he turned the Tammen charm on Bonfils, who put up the *Post*'s purchase price of $12,500. The two shook hands on a fifty-fifty partnership that never was put on paper but also never wavered during their lifetimes.

Bonfils was born of a gracious, middle-class Troy, Missouri, family of Corsican lineage, supposedly old friends of the Bonapartes. His father, Eugene Napoleon Bonfils, had been a newspaper editor, judge, and town banker with sufficient influence to get his son admitted to West Point—a classmate of John J. Pershing. But Bonfils withdrew before graduation, worked as a military academy teacher in Canon City, Colorado; a reporter in Troy, Missouri; a real estate speculator during the Oklahoma land rush; and then presumably made a pile in Kansas City's lottery business, unshackled by today's financial regulators. The *Kansas City Star*, not to put too good a face on matters, declared him "formerly a Kansas City real estate swindler." The two men were highly dissimilar, at least according to the reputations passed down by such chroniclers as Fowler, who cheerfully admitted that he did not let history get too much in the way of a good story. Tammen was short, plump, cheerful, openly compassionate, an imp of a man who was always deprecating his own motives and painting himself as a bumptious con man. Bonfils was taller, dashingly handsome, of military bearing, dour of personality and spartan of habit, and with a mercurial temper that inspired fear rather than friendship.

Within a decade or so, both men had been reviled by proper Denver, shot and grievously wounded in their offices, and were well known in the courts on matters of libel and assault. But they were also publishing a sensational success in circus-like promotion, circulation, and revenue, while at the same time flailing the politicians and the corporations in the best populist style. Bonfils as editor *and* publisher (a combined post that was a tradition for some years) and Tammen as business manager were shaping a newspaper that, as one critic put it, about half of Denver hated but all of Denver read.

III

When Bonfils and Tammen bought the *Evening Post* on October 28, 1895, it was an eight-page, failing paper with 6,000 claimed readers. But the paper turned a profit after two hard years, although the partners took no salary or dividends until 1908 when circulation at 83,000 had topped their local competitors combined. What the business world would now call their "marketing formula" was then just the sales instincts of two hustling journalism mavericks, their instinctive policies including a widely proclaimed political independence; a consistent focus on the average reader; considerable stress on economic development of not only a growing Denver but also its wider Western region; and an insistence on entertaining as well as informing the "people," who in that day were not yet tuned to broadcast or film.

Bonfils and Tammen pledged that the *Post* would be "free

from entanglements with political parties, corporations or special interests of any kind . . . free to do for the people and to be vigorously and unreservedly against whatever is against them." The *Post*, its first editorial promised,

> will devote special and çeaseless attention to the material interests of the state and to the development of her vast and varied resources. . . that more acres of land shall be brought under cultivation; that more exchanges of trade shall be made; that more mines shall be opened and profitably worked; that more mills and factories shall be built and more foundries and smelters put into blast; that capital shall command greater returns and labor secure larger rewards. . . . The cheer of prosperity shall reach a larger share of the people.

Sharp and tight-fisted, the partners were avid that this "cheer of prosperity" also find its way to themselves, but not before the paper could pay its way. They transferred slowly growing profits into hiring the best editorial and publishing talent available, and into the improved technologies then beginning to appear in the newspaper industry. They were the first Denver publishers to buy *all* the existing news services offered by telegraph, then the isolated city's major communications link to the world. They had the first comic strips west of the Mississippi. Three years after they started, they added a Sunday edition of sixteen pages, a monster for its time. They were reproducing in Denver the kind of mass-circulation metropolitan daily that had earlier taken root in coastal cities.

They focused the promotional and editorial direction of the *Post* toward the needs of "the people," who were their pledged target and who were immigrating to Denver in ever-greater numbers. According to Hosokawa, Tammen told his city editor:

> "You've seen a vaudeville show, haven't you? It's got every sort of act—laughs, tears, wonder, thrills, melodrama, tragedy, comedy, love, and hate. That's what I want you to give our readers." Bonfils phrased it another way: "Write the news for all of the people, not just the rich and important or those who think they are. If you are understood by the busy, simple folk, everybody will understand you."

"And always remember," Bonfils added, "we want Denver to talk about the *Post.*"

Just a few of *The Denver Post*'s early editorial crusades and promotions suggest why Denver, with surprising swiftness, began talking about the *Post:*

1. The paper launched a campaign against child labor in the big department stores, admittedly with most attention to those who refused to advertise in the *Post.* Bonfils and Tammen were no strangers to hard-ball tactics, and some of their business practices were to leave scars for generations. But, typically, their child-labor campaign also produced reform legislation from state politicians who began to pay the *Post* attention. Such pounding of the corporate interests dominated city politics, including competing newspapers such as the *Denver Times,* owned by financier David H. Moffat.

2. The private Denver Union Water Company, the *Post* reported, "served notice on the people through its official organ, the *Times,* that it would immediately begin to shut off the water from all those who had refused to pay its illegal and extortionate rates. . . . If anyone attempts or threatens to turn your water off, call at the office of the *Post* and we will see that your interests are protected." The paper headlined IMPURITY OF DENVER WATER, and the hammering ended in public ownership of the water system. Such stories as CONDUCTORS ROBBING LITTLE GIRLS OF THEIR HALF FARE TICKETS likewise afflicted the tramway system.

3. The *Post* thought coal prices were too high, so "today the *Post* will begin selling Northern coal at $3.50 a ton and will continue . . . until the Coal Trust sees fit to quit robbing the people." The paper later sold fish, apples, and potatoes direct to the people when prices were too high, to screams of "socialism" from affronted merchants.

4. When rabbits overran the northern plains, the *Post* organized massive hunts and trucked the dead animals to the city for distribution to the poor—in front of the newspaper. Also, mountain lion hunters trekked into the *Post*'s offices offering gunnysacks filled with heads for bounties as the paper sought to eliminate the cats from settled areas.

5. There was almost always a show at the *Post* building at 1544 Champa—Harry Houdini hanging from the roof, struggling in a straitjacket; high-wire artists prancing high above the street; Buffalo Bill, on the payroll, handing coins to children; and elephants from Tammen's own Sells-Floto circus nosing the newsboys. A floozie was hired to hide out in the Eden of Rocky Mountain National Park to be rediscovered as "Eve." The *Post* annual train trip for advertisers to Cheyenne began in 1908; pilgrimages were marshalled for the somewhat devout to the Mount of the Holy Cross in the Rockies.

A galaxy of talented people paraded in the rings of this journalistic circus, some of later national fame like Damon Runyon, Gene Fowler, Courtney Ryley Cooper, Burns Mantle, and George Creel, the World War I propaganda chief. Frances Wayne, Polly Pry, Nell Brinckley, Fay King, Wilbur Steele, Otto Floto, Lord Ogilvy, the nobly born British farm editor—these people and many more march at more colorful length through fine histories of the *Post* such as Bill Hosokawa's *Thunder in the Rockies*. The *Post*'s wares were wrapped in a screaming maze of red and black headlines, sledgehammer cartoons, illustrations, and a daily diet of news and opinion, most often mixed in the "yellow journalism" stew in vogue at the turn of the century. The famous *Post* city editor of the period, Josiah Ward, had taught a young William Randolph Hearst the business; and a mechanical genius, Billy Millburn, deployed the *Post*'s typographical artillery only after service with Joseph Pulitzer in New York. DOES IT HURT TO BE BORN? asked a front-page headline on one dull news day. The birth of a new way of newspapering apparently did not hurt very much for the people on the early *Denver Post*. They had a hell of a good time as Progressive-era reformers began to "rescue" Denver from its frontier-era civic management.

These mass-circulation newspapers of the Hearst-Pulitzer stamp were, in the absence of later broadcast media, giving their rising cities some sense of identity. Historian Gunther Barth in *City People* lists the metropolitan mass newspaper with the apartment house, the department store, the ball park, and the vaudeville house as new institutions contributing "more directly and extensively to the emergence of modern city culture than did the factory and political machine."

IV

During the first two decades of the twentieth century, Denver slowly matured as a regional city, and *The Denver Post,* founded in 1892, was growing up with the metropolis. From the turn of the century until World War I—which inextricably entangled provincial Colorado in a global web—city growth strained frontier political and social structures and attitudes.

The *Post* greeted the new century "with bounding hopes and intelligent confidence" but added that since the silver mining industry had been largely destroyed by Congress in the previous decade, the future depended on hard work by a people used to adversity. The paper's year-opening Glory Edition surveyed citizen desires for the forty-year-old city with such responses as beautification, burial of electric wires, cleaning much-manured streets, public cuspidors, larger jails, and better hospitals for the "lungers," druggies, and drunks crowding the city. Stories in the paper also included public ownership of the utilities; "home rule," which would free Denver from the governance of the state legislature; and more attention to juvenile delinquency. Even then, cleaner air was on the newspaper's agenda: "Enough smoke filled the air early this morning to make pedestrians believe they were in St. Louis or Pittsburgh."

Race relations were in a Neanderthal state; a brutal lynching of a young black man opened the century, and in 1907, shortly after the Pioneer Monument at the northwest corner of Broadway and Colfax was proposed, public outcry substituted Kit Carson for the Indian the sculptor had intended as its crown. In this era of violent labor-management wars, Denver was the home of William "Big Bill" Haywood, founder of the International Workers of the World, which radicalized the Western labor movement. And there was no question but that the civic institutions of Denver were dominated by those businessmen, or their sons, who had been running things since they had stepped off the stagecoaches. The *Post* blasted these corporate owners but was equally leery of labor radicals and callous to civil rights. Despite the economic bust of the mid-1890s, there was a good deal of optimism for the technological future, balanced, as always in the West, by nostalgia for the fading frontier. In Denver there were still Wild West elements in the brothels, the bars, the flophouses, and in the management instincts of the city's "establishment," obviously including Bonfils and Tammen.

But it was also a new world of cars, electrical inventions, and a faith in industrial machines. As to technological optimism, a *Post* poem by James Barton Adams, quoted in Robert Athearn's centennial history, *The Coloradans,* fantasized about the wonders ahead:

> Great ships of commerce traversing the air?
> Men upon wings flying 'round here and there?
> People all honest and square in their deals?
> Workingmen riding in automobiles?
> Women in Congress and cabinet hall?
> Fair mistress President over them all?
> Babies of new incubator design?
> Woman the oak and poor man but the vine?

As to the nostalgia for the Old West, the *Post* with the nation was transfixed by the death in Denver on January 10, 1917, of William "Buffalo Bill" Cody, long past his prime as scout and showman. The trim old veteran of battle, bottle, and boudoir was on the promotional payroll of the *Post.* When the sad day dawned, the paper proposed to the somewhat estranged widow that he be buried on Lookout Mountain, west of town. Buffalo Bill had yearned to rest in Wyoming, but Denver boosterism and bucks prevailed; Cody, and later his wife, were buried overlooking the city where he had ended—but not earned—his legend. The graves were later topped off with tons of cement to prevent Wyoming parties from stealing him back. Westerners took their heroes seriously in those days!

Gene Fowler, in the modest tones that characterized Bonfils and Tammen's *Post,* wrote after they had orchestrated the burial:

A day has passed. With it we have turned a page that cannot be rewritten. But it is all vivid and fresh in our minds—like the vast throng, the many thousands who began a journey yesterday morning to the summit of Lookout Mountain to an open grave. It was the tomb that was to receive the honored body of a modern knight errant, his escutcheon unsullied by selfishness, his record the history of the West. There where the winds of wide world meet, where the trails wind upward as if to lead to higher things, there they pressed the earth over William F. Cody . . . a pageant the like of which has never been viewed before. Indeed, 18,000 people had viewed the bier under the Capitol dome, and the world did mourn—for its dead dreams of the West as well as for its dead rascal.

Bonfils and Tammen were in the thick of all of this, castigating the corporate owners of the tramway and water company, blessing and damning the politicians, often in the same breath, getting shot and seriously wounded by a mad reader, and in and out of court on various libel matters. With a blow from behind, the pepper-pot Bonfils assaulted Senator Thomas M. Patterson, the owner of the *Rocky Mountain News,* and paid a fifty-dollar fine for his ever-excessive temper. But mad or calm, the paper made money hand over fist and lapped all of its rivals in circulation.

The *Post* editorialized on various sides of various issues, always with an eye to the development of Colorado, particularly of its water, roads, and tourism, and most always with a suspicion of politicians. For example, it was alternately in and out of camp with Mayor Robert Speer, the dominant city political force of the era, who befriended both corporations and madams, and who enraged the Progressive reformers. But Speer also built the parks and parkways, planted the trees, cleaned the streets and sewers, and had the vision for such amenities as mountain parks and the Civic Center, both of which later transformed Denver. A year before Speer's death in 1917, the *Post* opined, "Speerism has done more to debase and debauch and belittle and retard and to dwarf Denver than any other curse that has befallen us." However, a week after his death it wrote, "His vision was broad, his activities effective, forceful, and unceasing. He was the creator of the City Beautiful." Amid rapid change, it was hard to make up editorial minds about what constituted civic virtue.

V

The Denver Post, from the World War I era, prospered with a style of journalism its critics called "yellow" and worse. Its driving owners, Bonfils and Tammen, continued to mix their colorful personalities, super salesmanship, and mercurial, populistic political independence in a razzle-dazzle blend of news and opinion, a blend that many national journalists felt challenged their growing professional ethic of "objectivity."

The dividing line between the *Post* and its owners was always blurred. In a telling 1914 example, the *Post* opposed a twenty-year extension of the city's water supply franchise to the private Denver Union Water Company. The *Post* wanted municipal ownership. The *Post*'s campaign was so heated that Bonfils went to the courthouse as plaintiff in a lawsuit against the water company. An opposing attorney drew a revolver. The *Post* editor lunged with fists and disarmed the enemy, but a court subsequently found the lawyer not guilty of assault because he had received "the worse of the encounter." The franchise extension was defeated, with the *Post* inviting readers down to the Champa Street plant for the election returns, and to be serenaded by Vocalino, the siren of the newspaper-owned Sells-Floto circus. *Post* historian Hosokawa concludes that "under the flamboyance and whoop-de-do, despite the bitterly emotional personal attacks, there had been genuine accomplishment. The rejection of the franchise led to municipal ownership of Denver's water system . . . the key to orderly development of water resources, perhaps the largest single factor in municipal growth on the arid eastern slope of the Rockies."

The newspaper's editorial positions were still given and taken quite personally after World War I when labor troubles were widespread. On August 4, 1920, during a tramway strike which the city with *Post* support was trying to break, an enraged mob invaded the paper on Champa Street. It smashed furniture and typewriters, rolled some newsprint out onto a street jammed with spectators, and set some fires which a copyboy stamped out. Damage was minimal, and the invasion made good copy the next day. In the postwar era, when growing immigration and the scare about the Russian Revolution had turned much of the United States into a hunting ground for extremists, Colorado and the *Post* were no models of civil rights virtue. During the war the paper had lashed out at German-American citizens; afterwards, during labor troubles, it called for "a necessary and timely rebuke to the anarchists, to bolshevists, and to the foreign labor leaders who have come to this country to destroy it." In April 1920, a few months before the tramway strike invasion, a *Post* front-page screamer even announced that the Reds were planning to overthrow the United States government on May Day.

Thus, when the Ku Klux Klan emerged in its greatest western strength in Colorado in 1921 (and by 1924 had elected a governor and a mayor, to say nothing of a majority of the state House of Representatives), the newspaper's at-best grudging toleration of an increasingly diverse population was put to the test. (The color of the era is contained in *Denver,* John Dunning's excellent novel about Denver and the *Post.*) Happily the *Post* rose to the occasion when the Klan-supported governor, Clarence J. Morley, tried to evict the warden of the state penitentiary and pardon prisoners wholesale. After a rambunctious campaign, Morley left office discredited and unsuccessfully sued the paper for libel. The Klan's influence in Colorado waned.

While wrestling these urban dragons, the *Post* also developed its tradition of state and regional development. "*The Denver Post,*" wrote the not-too-modest Bonfils, "is the greatest market place in the West. . . . Denver is destined by nature to be the great metropolis of mid-America, the capital and business hub of the most American part of America. . . . *The Denver Post* is dedicated to building up Denver and Colorado and the Rocky Mountain region."

Despite earlier wars with David H. Moffat, the banker-dreamer of a railroad over the Rockies, the *Post* after his death supported the Moffat Tunnel to take his rails under the Great Divide, and, incidentally, to return water to the Front Range. The newspaper, with others, shepherded the necessary legislation through the Colorado General Assembly. The massive public works project jumped financial and political hurdles of all kinds and was finally completed in 1927, sixteen years after Moffat's death. The *Post* celebrated with a "sowbelly" dinner for the Advertising Clubs of the World at a 900-foot table in the tunnel's bore.

Several other events of the 1920s illustrate the highly personal character of *Post* history in this era. Bonfils, proclaiming innocence and never formally sanctioned, became involved in the Teapot Dome scandal in Wyoming, facing a U.S. Senate inquiry about a payment received from oilman Harry Sinclair that coincided with the dropping of a *Post* campaign against government oil leases. Subsequent criticism from the American Society of Newspaper Editors led to Bonfils's resignation in what was quite a newspaper industry flap in its time.

And in a less dramatic but far more telling setback for Bonfils, Harry H. Tammen, the fun-loving and compassionate super salesman who had been Bonfils's indefatigable and trusting partner since 1895, died of cancer on July 19, 1924, putting an end to the partnership that keynoted the newspaper's first era. When the sight of one eye faded in his final illness, Tammen put a patch over it saying, "Read *The Denver Post.*" Tammen explained that "the eye quit working for me so I put it to work for the *Post.*" A multimillionaire from the *Post*'s success, Tammen and his wife Agnes gave much of their wealth to endow Denver's famous Children's Hospital, and the hospital eventually held a significant share of *Post* stock from the Tammen estate, the bone in a landmark ownership contention forty years later. Tammen's death had a deep impact on Bonfils, who, acquaintances said, lost not only a partner but a restraining influence on his impulsive temperament. "More than half of me is gone," said Bonfils. "I shall never get over it, for Harry and I were so necessary to each other."

But Bonfils went on alone. The *Post* continued its vigorous growth and regional championship, including an attempt to organize an economic development League of Rocky Mountain States. Bonfils was so proud of his paper that he saw nothing amiss in offering, on the front page, its editorship to President

Calvin Coolidge on the latter's retirement in 1928. However, the dominating tone of Bonfils's final years was set by the *Post*'s first tangle with the Scripps Howard national newspaper group which in November 1926 bought the *Rocky Mountain News*. The ensuing competition, his family always believed, was a contributing factor in Bonfils's unexpected death on February 2, 1933, just as the Great Depression was getting a grip on Denver.

VI

This first century of *Denver Post* history has seen the American communications environment shift from one in which newspapers of all hues fought no-holds-barred in all cities, to the present, in which Denver is one of the few metropolitan cities with any competing dailies at all. When *The Denver Post* was founded in 1892, the *Rocky Mountain News*, the *Express*, the *Times*, and the *Republican* were locked in conflict without the competitive annoyance of radio or television broadcasts. Within a very few years, the *Post* had outdistanced all the others combined in both circulation and revenue, and only the *News* remained a serious challenger. This vigorous competition (sometimes but not always meriting the "war" label now so beloved of national media observers) between *The Denver Post* and the *Rocky Mountain News* became a major theme of community history which continues to this day.

The *News*, when locally owned, had bounced between owners ever since Denver's beginning in 1859 when it was edited by the famous community builder, William N. Byers. He withdrew after nineteen years to be replaced by Col. John Arkins. Then, after fourteen years, the *News* went to Sen. Thomas M. Patterson, a prominent Democratic and populist political figure; this was in 1892 when *The Denver Post* was born, some say because Patterson deserted the national Democratic administration. Patterson sold in twenty-one years in 1913 to a Chicago publisher, John Shaffer, who in turn sold in thirteen years to the Scripps Howard national newspaper group, the present owners. Both the Patterson and the Shaffer ownerships of the *News* were bedeviled and eventually beaten by fierce confrontation with the flamboyant news and business tactics of Bonfils and Tammen. The *Post*'s relations with Patterson were fairly calm at first, both papers being populist in tone and mostly opposed to the business establishment then dominating Denver. Indeed, in 1900, when a disgruntled lawyer shot and nearly killed Bonfils and Tammen in their office (popularly nicknamed "The Bucket of Blood" for its red walls and feisty atmosphere), the *News* editorialized that "Bonfils and Tammen have many faults. They have not published an ideal paper. They in many instances violate accepted newspaper ethics. But they are brave men, and in public matters stood mainly for the right. . . . They are generous of heart, impulsive and irascible. Many men can be better spared from the community than they." The *Post* soon reciprocated by endorsing Patterson for senator.

But the temporary collegiality could not survive the personalized business atmosphere of the next decade, best summarized in a Christmas 1907 *News* editorial which accused Bonfils of blackmailing businessmen for advertising revenue. There followed a famous incident in which the pugilistic Bonfils knocked Patterson down, for which he paid a fifty-dollar assault fine a few months later. Patterson could not substantiate his blackmail charges in court, and Bonfils did not sue for libel. Most of Denver sided with Patterson in sympathy but with Bonfils by reading his paper.

John C. Shaffer, who has left Denver a monument in the old Ken Caryl ranch house, was the next *News* owner. He also purchased the *Times*, which the *News* now owned, and the morning *Republican*, so he had the *News* in the morning delivery field and the merged *Times-Republican* in the afternoon, facing the *Post* and the wobbly *Express*. The *Post* editorialized that the *"News* and the *Times* are unsatisfactory as newspapers, caring nothing for the public good, being violent corporation organs which cater to the few instead of to the public as a whole." By the time of Harry Tammen's death in 1924, the *Post* had clearly withstood Shaffer's ownership of the *News/Times* and the Chicagoan was looking for a sale. He found his buyer in Roy W. Howard, who on November 22, 1926, purchased the *News* and the *Times*, and the still wobbly *Express,* for his growing Scripps Howard chain. Howard merged the *Times* and *Express* into a new *Denver Evening News* for head-on competition with the *Post,* leaving the *Rocky Mountain News* to morning delivery.

The new version of the *News* immediately defended its elimination of the other Denver papers. "We believe that the dictatorship of Denver's newspaper field by *The Denver Post* would be nothing less than a blight . . . a sinister journalistic situation." The national journalism press, as exemplified by *Editor and Publisher,* saw the Scripps Howard entry into Denver as something of a crusade to relieve the city of its "cloud of contemptible journalism," referring to Bonfils and Tammen's "yellow" tactics.

How would Bonfils, without his sidekick Tammen, react to the direct challenge by a powerful national group? He swiftly established the first morning edition in the *Post's* history. *The Morning Post* came out on January 3, 1927, and for two years the town was treated to an all-out newspaper slugfest the likes of which it has not seen before or since. Ad rate cuts, sensational stories and display, flamboyant promotions, merchandise premiums, the introduction by the *Post* of rotogravure printing—all played a part in the two-year mud wrestle. But it cost both sides too much money for the times. In 1926, before this first real *Post-News* "war," *Post* profits had been $1,171,000; in 1927 they were $384,000. Scripps Howard was losing profits, too, so by the end of 1928 both sides were thinking of peace. The *Post* was still overwhelmingly dominant in the afternoons, and its new morning edition had climbed to within striking distance of the *News.*

Thus Howard called a summit meeting with Bonfils; each sold their weaker papers to the other; and Denver again had only two papers, the *News* in the morning and the *Post* in the afternoon. Scripps Howard lost about $3 million, the *Post* about $2 million, and as the *Post* business manager then observed, "in this so-called newspaper war, while the spectators cheered from the sidelines, the contestants lost about $5 million. . . . We expect that [now] both of us will spend more time in building up and less in tearing down."

Thus ended the first real *Post-News* "war," though there was to be one more immediate round, to say nothing of skirmishes through the next half century. In August 1932 the *News* printed a front-page story in which a Democratic politician told a political meeting that Bonfils was a "rattlesnake . . . a public enemy [who] has left the trail of a slimy serpent across Colorado for 30 years . . . the contemptible dog of Champa Street." Bonfils, incensed at what he believed the stimulation and overplay of the story, sued the *News* for libel. The *News* launched an intensive investigation into Bonfils's personal background, and hearings and depositions portended virulent litigation. Then Bonfils, aged seventy-two, suddenly died on February 2, 1933, of an ear infection that had led to acute inflammation of the brain. The libel suit died with him, and *The Denver Post* entered the Great Depression without either of the journalistic salesmen who had made both its fortune and its special brand of fame.

VII

When Tammen died in 1924, his half of *The Denver Post's* stock, valued then at $5 million, went to his wife, Agnes Reid Tammen, and to a trust for the Children's Hospital. The Tammens had no direct heirs, and by endowing the hospital they had chosen to make the city's children their own: "It's better to give life to a child than to others, because a child means more to the community than anything else. I want the child who hasn't a name to have just the same tender care as a child that doesn't have to worry about what it's called," said the son of German immigrants who had left home as a teenager.

The fifth of the *Post's* stock held by the hospital was a philanthropic gold mine, for the newspaper, despite its reputation for sensationalism, continued to be one of the most prosperous in the country: In the twenty hectic economic years from 1925 to the end of World War II, gross revenues ranged from $4.5 to $6 million annually and profit margins from 20 to 36 percent. These high earnings, especially during the Depression years and before high federal income taxation, laid the base for substantial philanthropies from *Post* owners to the community in subsequent years, although at times it might have been better for more of the earnings to have been plowed back into the paper. Several opportunities to buy out the opposition or expand into broadcasting were bypassed in the transition years following Bonfils's and Tammen's death.

Bonfils, tightfisted and autocratic, did not have a wide public reputation for community concern. But he, too, thought about the future of Denver and its western region. In 1927 he set up the Frederick G. Bonfils Foundation "for the betterment of mankind. Those five words are the ruling and governing spirit of the Foundation. The idea is as broad as the world, yet I have in mind my special love for our people of this great inter-mountain territory, particularly the people of . . . Colorado and Wyoming." One of the early benefactions of this foundation was the Colorado Boulevard land on which University Hospital now stands, and eventually it was to provide Denver with its hallmark Center for the Performing Arts.

When Bonfils died at age seventy-two in 1933, he was sur-vived by two daughters, May and Helen, and by his elderly and frail widow, Belle. May Bonfils had affronted her father by what he considered an undesirable marriage, so his interest turned increasingly to his younger daughter, Helen. Upon his death, control of the newspaper, for the first time without a founding partner at the helm, passed to a board made up of Agnes Tammen, Helen Bonfils, William C. Shepherd, who had served the partners loyally in various editorial roles for two decades, and several titular supernumeraries. May and Helen Bonfils were to become bitterly estranged in the next few years in litigating their father's will. Helen became increasingly promi-nent in control of the paper while May was left to develop a personal social court in the suburbs.

There followed what *Post* historian Hosokawa has called a period of hibernation. Shepherd, who took over as president, editor, and publisher, had joined Bonfils and Tammen in 1908 and was managing editor from 1912 until Bonfils's death. The only kind of newspaper he knew how to publish was the one "Bon and Tam" had designed—sensational and highly opinion-ated with news and comment mixed on every page. "In the twelve full years of Shepherd's management, " Hosokawa writes,

"*The Post* showed a net profit of $18,452,000, of which all but $302,000 was distributed as dividends. . . . Nothing was put aside for future expansion, or to modernize or replace the aging physical plant built in 1907."

When Shepherd took over at age fifty-eight, at the height of the Depression with the dusty windstorms on the eastern plains already blowing many of his readers out of state, radio was emerging as a competitor to newspapers for the advertising dollar. And, in Hosokawa's summary, "a people made cynical by the Depression's grinding pressures were less inclined to be enchanted by the *Post*'s traditional showmanship, tantrums, and hyperbole in red ink. . . . Tammen and Bonfils, with their intuition for what interested people, would not have hesitated to change with the times. But Shepherd could not for he was not an innovator but a caretaker."

Of interest because of Bonfils's and Tammen's paternalistic influence over their editorial staff was the first American Newspaper Guild labor contract signed on August 4, 1938, after the famous partners were dead. It called for $22.50 a week for beginning reporters and $40.00 for those with three years of experience. A five-day week was called for as soon as possible, the contract being concluded only after a bitter struggle and pressure from John L. Lewis and the United Mine Workers. Shepherd was strongly anti–New Deal, and the paper scoffed not only at Franklin D. Roosevelt's reforms but at the reported international threat in the rise of Adolf Hitler in Germany and the Japanese military in Manchuria. When war broke, the surprised *Post* was frozen in newsprint quotas well below its normal needs. Meanwhile its competitor, the *Rocky Mountain News,* had gone to a tabloid format and was picking up circulation after nearly selling out to the *Post* in the late 1930s.

Agnes Tammen, one of the strong women of the *Post,* maintained a close interest in the paper at all times. Her counterpart, Helen Bonfils, was developing a professional career as an actress and producer, living part of the time in New York, and was not at this time as directly involved in the paper. She had been married since 1936 but was without children. She was intensely interested in supporting Denver theater and seemed to many to be dedicating her life to improving her father's piratical image in the eyes of Denver. Among her early and favorite philanthropies were the free summer *Post* operettas in Cheesman Park; various Catholic charities, including the building of Holy Ghost Church for downtown's denizens; the Belle Bonfils Memorial Blood Bank; and many smaller benefactions. "Miss Helen's" generosity as well as her fierce defense of her father's reputation had become a Denver byword by the wartime 1940s.

World War II transformed Denver and the West, and in the process set the stage for transforming the *Post* as the clearly dominant regional newspaper. There was a tremendous postwar influx of readers both more demanding and more culturally diverse than those who had been satisfied with the news standards of an isolated regional city. Bonfils and Tammen had put their stamp on the *Post* for some forty years, and on their transitional heirs for another ten. But Helen Bonfils and lawyer E. Ray Campbell, who had succeeded Agnes Tammen in control of that interest after her death in 1942, realized that the old ways would not guarantee the newspaper's survival as Denver moved toward becoming a more sophisticated metropolis. They went looking for a "revolutionary" new leader, and in 1946 got as much, if not more, than they bargained for in the person of Palmer "Ep" Hoyt, who ruled the paper into the 1970s.

Helen Bonfils confers over the Employee Stock Trust. From left to right are Joe W. Bruce, Earl Moore, Ivor Jones, and I. M. Rosenblatt.

Palmer Hoyt

A NEW RESPECTABILITY
The Legacy of Helen Bonfils and Palmer Hoyt

I

In the depressed 1930s, *The Denver Post*'s editorial policy was provincially suspicious of the increased federal involvement in Denver and the West that was driven by the depression-fighting New Deal. In 1934 the *Post* backed the conservative and isolationist Edwin C. "Big Ed" Johnson for a second term as governor and chortled that his election had "halted the Red march." It was similarly doubtful about national intervention overseas. As President Roosevelt rallied the country against totalitarianism in Europe and Asia, the *Post* said, "If another war is coming, let's wait for it to arrive this time instead of going out to meet it." These attitudes toward national change mirrored those of a Denver which journalist John Gunther called "Olympian, passive, and inert . . . probably the most self-sufficient, isolated and self-contained city in the world."

But the cocoon was cracking. The tremendous growth of federal investment in the West, as a result not only of the New Deal but also of World War II defense expansion, and the surge of new population spurred by this investment, meant to Denver and its Mountain West region changes more profound than any since the first miners and town boosters rushed into the wilderness. The resulting population growth, as noted by historian Gerald D. Nash in *The American West Transformed,* brought more than eight million newcomers into the trans-Mississippi West, including more than three million servicemen and women, many of whom after the war settled in the promised land. It was no

wonder, he stated, that the migration created new social problems in Western cities—of housing, health, transportation, education, and social services. And since the Great Migration of
1941 to 1945 included significant minority groups, including
blacks and Mexicans, the new population boom also created new
racial and ethnic tensions.

The editorial attitudes of the old *Denver Post* were ill-tuned to
this Great Migration, or to the nation's sudden dive into global
affairs. As an example, after the Japanese attack on Pearl
Harbor, the *Post* lashed out at Japanese-American citizens. "The
war between the United States and Japan," the *Post* opinion
column "That's That" said in 1943, "is not merely a war between
the American and Jap governments. IT IS A FIGHT TO THE
DEATH BETWEEN THE AMERICAN PEOPLE AND THE JAP
PEOPLE." From the Heart Mountain, Wyoming, relocation
center where some of the West Coast's Japanese-Americans
were interned, the *Heart Mountain Sentinel* responded, "The
most notorious of yellow journals has found a convenient tool
to promote its anti-Democratic, anti–New Deal campaign. . . .
We protest the viciously editorialized headlines coldly calculated
to inflame public opinion against loyal American citizens whose
only crime was that of being born with Japanese faces."

Post historian Hosokawa, himself an alumnus of Heart Mountain mistreatment and in the postwar era a distinguished editor
at the *Post,* recorded the newspaper's awakening to the need to
change with the tumultuous times. When, in 1942, the capable
Agnes Reid Tammen died, she was succeeded in control of the
Tammen interests by Attorney E. Ray Campbell as vice president
of the newspaper. Hosokawa writes that Campbell realized the
Post might become a "dinosaur doomed because it could not
adjust to changing times. His business instincts told him that if
the newspaper was to survive, its dividend policies would have
to be changed; the directors would have to stop giving it away
a bit at a time to some very wealthy heirs." Campbell and Helen
Bonfils were already thinking of replacing William C. Shepherd
when he suddenly retired.

Thus in early 1946, just after the war's end, Campbell began
the search that brought Palmer Hoyt to Denver and to a twenty-

five-year reign. As Hosokawa viewed it, Campbell felt the *Post* "needed a Westerner as its editor. . . . He wanted someone with roots in the West, who understood the West and its aspirations." He also wanted someone young enough to give the *Post* twenty years of service, and with a background of successful newspaper leadership and management. For, Campbell believed, "'A newspaper cannot be run like any other business. Unless it keeps its driving spirit, its soul, its unceasing quest for the new, it can quite rapidly fade and disappear.' Whether he knew it or not, he was seeking an editor who could restore *The Post*'s old color and flamboyance without the venality."

Hoyt, then forty-nine, was a burly former ranch hand and pulp fiction writer, raised in the West. He had risen from sportswriter and movie critic to editor and publisher of the *Portland Oregonian,* in the process thoroughly reviving that family newspaper. He had national stature as an editor and had been director of the U.S. Office of War Information for a brief period. His reputation was that of an editorial writer to the core who inspired great devotion but who did not easily share command, even with owners. His news credo, a world apart from that of the old Bonfils *Post,* was "PRINT THE NEWS AS FAIRLY AS YOU CAN; COMMENT ON THE NEWS ADEQUATELY, AND NEVER LET THE TWO FUNCTIONS MIX."

That credo at first made Hoyt think he did not want the new job. As he later told his biographer, Mort Stern, "Because of their procedures . . . they had no editorial page [dropped in 1911] . . . [and] were running their editorials in the news. . . . They had, if not a conscious blackbook, at least people and causes that were not mentioned." Hoyt told Helen Bonfils and Campbell that "I couldn't think of running a paper that didn't have an editorial page . . . that had a blacklist as to people and causes . . . that didn't have the proper physical equipment. I said I felt that the *Post* was a sort of a practical, everyday *Police Gazette* operated and displayed in a sensational fashion long since out-of-date." But despite the radical changes Hoyt obviously represented, he was hired on his own terms to become editor and publisher of the *Post* on February 20, 1946. With the promotional flare of a Bonfils and Tammen, the new boss soon labeled

the *Post* the "Voice of the Rocky Mountain Empire" and began
to bestride his domain in imperial style, to the irritation of some
of Denver's old guard and, it later developed, to the chagrin of
Helen Bonfils, who thought of her father as the only emperor
the *Post* would ever need.

II

The Denver Post, along with the city and Western region it
mirrors, underwent the most fundamental changes in their
interdependent history as the result of World War II. And as
change transformed the region, the managements of Denver
and Mountain West institutions adapted—some alertly, some
grudgingly, some not at all. Among the most alert was Hoyt at
The Denver Post. He took over a newspaper that had lost the
vigor if not the sensationalistic formulas or substantial profits of
its dominant founders. Helen Bonfils, fifty-seven, respected for
her philanthropies, her professional theatrical career, and for
her fierce devotion to her controversial father's memory, saw
the *Post* as "papa's monument—dynamic, protean, and strong
with the strength of a virile man." She must have seen some such
characteristics in the thoroughly masculine, almost swashbuck-
ling Hoyt. One lure, she told *Newsweek,* was his "vision for the
West, the greatest vision I have seen since Papa has gone."

Papa's monument thus entrusted to Hoyt in 1946 was a
newspaper of 187,801 daily and 306,664 Sunday circulation,
with gross revenues of $6,062,000 and a 21.97 percent net profit
of $1,332,000, of which, as was the *Post* custom, a substantial
$1,200,000 was paid out in dividends. The editorial product was
sleepy, isolationist, and reactionary; the staff underpaid and cut
to the bone by wartime stringencies; the newsprint supply low;
and the 1907 mechanical plant held together by baling wire. The
paper was still dominated by red front pages and screamer
headlines, circus typography, opinionated news coverage, and
unbalanced editorial comment mixed with the news. Its reputation among newspaper professionals was that of a Neanderthal
throwback. A loyal and hard-working staff was keeping the

paper dominant among Denver readers by putting it out the way Frederick Bonfils would have wanted. Such was the mercurial magnetism of an editor/owner thirteen years dead, his memory jealously guarded by a vigilant and astute daughter.

The newspaper revolution that Hoyt produced in a few short years has been summarized elsewhere for students of the trade—colorfully in Hosokawa's *Thunder in the Rockies,* more academically in an unpublished University of Denver doctoral thesis by Mort Stern. Briefly summarized, these were its major elements:

1. Introduction to the *Post* of the philosophy that news and editorial comment were not to be mixed, even by the indirect games that newspersons play. News coverage and its display in headlines and placement were to be meticulously fair. Unconscious or actual news blackouts of Bonfils's enemies were eliminated. All races were to be given fair treatment, in both employment and coverage. Hoyt meant it, and as an old reporter, city editor, and copyreader, he knew how to enforce it.

2. The *Post* was soon named the "Voice of the Rocky Mountain Empire," building on an old Bonfils recognition that the Mountain West and the city were umbilically linked. "An area such as this needs a voice, a spokesman," Hoyt told Stern. "The *Post* has always been more than just a city newspaper." The new editor had herded sheep and wrangled cattle, and consistently supported, even at the very conservative *Oregonian,* water and tourism development. Reporters were dispatched to all corners of the West, notably the since-famous Robert W. "Red" Fenwick, who became the *Post*'s ambassador to hamlet and horse.

3. The newspaper's region became the world, as well as the city and its hinterland. Hoyt was a liberal internationalist with wide acquaintance in Washington, D.C. He sent reporters abroad and throughout the land, established a strong Washington bureau, and himself was active on national commissions for air policy and Radio Free Europe. At one point in his early years, he was in Washington for a few days in each of twenty successive weeks.

4. To buttress and eventually supplant an aging and tired management staff, Hoyt imported the "Oregon gang" of young disciples from the *Oregonian,* notably Charles R. Buxton, who

became Hoyt's right hand in the newspaper's transformation as business manager, and later as Hoyt's successor. Hoyt implanted his imports into the *Post* hierarchy by osmosis rather than surgery; he never fired someone he could transfer or promote into another spot. "Do your job and get a better job" was the dictum. He made friends with everyone, and paid attention to such details as restoring the doors to the men's room stalls, removed by previous management to discourage malingering.

5. A personal hands-on role in the community was integral to Hoyt's philosophy. A publisher, he said, must be known and respected in the community for his newspaper to be so known and respected. Accordingly, he made speech after speech and delved directly into local politics, the most notable early result being the replacement in 1947 of the venerable Mayor Ben Stapleton by the young war veteran Quigg Newton, ending a city hall regime that had controlled politics since the 1920s.

6. Plans were implemented for a new plant at Fifteenth and California. When the $6 million plant, paid for by revenues diverted from the lush dividend stream, was dedicated in 1950, newspaper dignitaries from throughout the country testified to the modernization that had taken place in four short years.

7. Probably most important in Hoyt's mind, a modern editorial page was established in 1946, the first in the *Post* since 1911. This was vital to give both the visual separation of news and opinion and the "Voice of the Rocky Mountain Empire" that Hoyt thought essential to reviving the newspaper's professional respectability. For the ensuing forty-five years these editorial pages endured as the most lasting monument to the Hoyt revolution, one that vaulted *The Denver Post* from one of the most notorious to one of the most respected regional newspapers.

III

The earlier *Post* had run separate editorials from 1895 to 1911, then abandoned them for large-type, front-page opinions under the heading "So the People May Know." The *Post* frequently also used front-page cartoons to advance its political position. It also published an unsigned column of political opinion, "That's That," which was widely perceived but not formally described as representing the newspaper's opinion. Some twenty years later, in insisting on separating news from opinion, Hoyt was responding to a new ethic of American journalism that had strengthened steadily since the turn of the century. The highly personal, biased journalism of the Hearst-type publisher had gone out of style.

Hoyt wrote the first editorial on the new page on May 19, 1946. It set the tone of the *Post*'s effort in the following years to become both more forceful and more balanced. "This page," Hoyt wrote in the left-hand column under the paper's masthead,

> will present the divergent views of nationally known columnists and public figures, and of . . . readers. In this, the editorial column, *The Post* will speak for and to Denver, Colorado and the Rocky Mountain Empire. In this column you will find the views of *The Post*. Those views will not be found elsewhere; not in the news columns, which will present the daily world, national, regional, and local scenes clearly, factually, and objectively; not in the signed columns which will present the thinking and ideas of the individual writers regardless of whether or not they conflict with those of *The Post*.

In another break with tradition, Hoyt established a more vigorous and balanced letters-to-the-editor tradition, the "Open Forum." The older *Post* had run a forum on Sundays consisting only of letters overwhelmingly of the Bonfils-Tammen viewpoint. But Hoyt told the readers that "you are invited to express your views in the open forum which will run today and every day." The voice of the people is the voice of the sovereign, a theme reminiscent of Bonfils and Tammen introducing their *Post* in 1895.

Hoyt, in his 1946 editorial, staked out his basic concept of newspaper operation and of its role as a regional voice. The editorial page was added, he wrote, "to fulfill this newspaper's concept of its basic function: namely to print the news fairly and accurately and to comment adequately thereon." As to the region, he saw it as "an economic empire of untold wealth and of vast importance to the United States and to the world. Denver, its capital, is a city of certain destiny. To help Denver and the Rocky Mountain Empire keep their appointment with destiny is the prime responsibility of the *Post*." Its goals thus laid out, the *Post* editorial page began to seek them. The next day it began campaigns for a new sports stadium, an auditorium "in keeping with necessities and dignities of a modern city," a traffic improvement survey, and more copious and legible street signs. Poor street signs were a special irritant to newcomer Hoyt, to which Mayor Stapleton reacted, "If they were good enough for the son-of-a-bitch to find his way into town by them, he can find his way out." There was a good deal of resentment among the Denver establishment at Hoyt's pressure for change and his perceptions of destiny and empire.

Fred Colvig, the first of the new editorial page editors, set a fast pace in wide-ranging personal investigations by page staff; in fact, he was killed on July 12, 1949, when his airliner went down on an investigative trip to Indonesia, then fighting for its independence from the Dutch. Colvig was followed as editor of the page by Edwin Hoyt, Jr., 1949–51; Robert W. Lucas, 1952–58; Mort Stern, 1958–65 and 1971–73; James Idema, 1965–71; Robert Pattridge, 1973–77; Bill Hosokawa, 1977–83; Chuck Green, 1983–88 and 1990 to the present; and Carl Miller, 1988–89. They reported to the editor and publisher of the newspaper, the job being combined in one person during the Hoyt era as it had been under Bonfils.

The *Post* had a long tradition of vigorous political cartooning, but national recognition was delayed until the post–World War II makeover when the cartoon was permanently lodged on the editorial page. Two cartoonists won Pulitzer prizes for their work, Paul Conrad in 1963 (though the award was received after he went to the *Los Angeles Times*), and Pat Oliphant in 1967. Mike Keefe, a later cartoonist, received both the Sigma Delta Chi and Headliners Club national cartoon awards in 1986.

Then and now, there is considerable mystery among readers about how a newspaper editorial page operates. Under the new *Post* system, all points of view were to be represented. The paper's own viewpoint was to be recognized only in the editorial column. This viewpoint was forged by interplay between editorial writers, page editors, and the public, with reference to the editor and publisher for final decision when necessary. There was a strict separation between the working staffs of the editorial page and the news gathering operations, to keep the human pressures of editorial opinion away from the news columns and vice versa. This insulation has stayed remarkably intact over the years.

By rough count, some ten thousand *Post* editorial pages have appeared since 1946, featuring a clash of opinion about political endorsements, public works developments, ethnic struggles, national wars and scandals, international hostilities and cooperations, human victories and defeats. A sketch such as this can examine only a few of the major issues thus addressed, to highlight the complex process by which a newspaper, while doing its main job of reporting the news, also tries to help its city, state, and region develop and improve. If the Hoyt *Post* had a single theme, it was Denver's destiny. "Destiny" seems an overblown word to journalists of the 1990s, but to Hoyt, a genuine Western booster, it was manifest that Denver, Colorado, and the Mountain West were moving toward a sparkling future. The *Post*'s editorial page in examining basic community issues was intended to help guide the community to that future.

IV

The Denver Post's relationship to the mayors of Denver has been a sometimes rough, sometimes smooth thread in the history of both city and newspaper. One significant example was the election of a thirty-five-year-old war veteran, Quigg Newton, in May 1947, the smokiest signal yet to Denver's old guard that the aftermath of World War II meant massive change. Newton ended the grip on City Hall of Mayor Stapleton, who with the solid support of the business establishment had served except for one term since 1923. The young lawyer's election was in part due to Hoyt. The *Post* has always endorsed candidates for City

Hall with mixed success, seldom allowing its passions of election day to influence editorial attitudes the morning after. But Hoyt had a hands-on philosophy about the role of a newspaper publisher in city politics, and began editorial page criticism of City Hall almost from the day he arrived in Denver. The old mayor had served Denver long and well, but after the war, at age seventy-seven, was obviously at risk to a youthful new broom. Hoyt's old friend, Supreme Court Justice William O. Douglas, suggested his former law clerk and Denver native, Newton, and Hoyt spread the word. Endorsed by the *Post* as promising an "alert and progressive administration," Newton won the election with 57 percent of the vote, Stapleton finishing third.

Newton served two terms and his regime, solidly backed by the *Post,* was responsible for many new features in Denver municipal government that remain strengths today. Among such achievements listed by George V. Kelly in his *The Old Gray Mayors of Denver* were a new Community Relations Commission; the first central planning office; 2,300 public housing units; a master traffic control system; reorganization of the police department; the Career Service Authority; and thorough reform of the city's financial system. Not the least of the Newton-era contributions was a cadre of future civil servants such as Bruce Rockwell, Hugh Catherwood, Ralph Radetsky, Dr. Solomon Kauvar, Tom Campbell, and Leonard Campbell.

When Newton stepped down in 1955, Denver was treated to its first "runoff" election, the voters having just decreed that a mayor must henceforth have a majority, not just a plurality, of the vote. It was also the first televised election, pitting an incumbent two-term Democratic district attorney, Bert Keating, against a two-term Republican state senator, Will F. Nicholson, in the presumably nonpartisan race. Keating, with an entrenched political machine, was the strong favorite in the early polls but led only 45.8 percent to Nicholson's 44.46 percent in the first election, the latter having staged a four-and-a-half-hour televised "Mayorathon" to help close the gap. A last-minute malicious attempt was made to link Nicholson to an anti-Catholic smear of Keating, but "Big Nick" was able to prove innocence and won the runoff by a scant 820 votes from the last twenty precincts counted. The *Post* had endorsed Nicholson all the way as "most likely to carry on city government in the non-partisan spirit of the Charter" and because he promised a more adequate water supply for Denver. As with Newton, Hoyt maintained close personal contact with Nicholson, whose friendship with President Dwight D. Eisenhower helped produce the U.S. Air Force Academy and more transmountain water for the booming metropolis.

Nicholson left office after one term, and the *Post*, in 1959, endorsed both Republican Richard Batterton and Democrat George Cavender in the final election, stating that in either case "the city would be in good hands [but facing] problems of explosive growth, metropolitan disorder, suburban antagonism, a city budget that is barebones. . . . Their job is [to] unite a fragmented business community and an apathetic and suspicious public." Batterton won election by about 8,000 votes but his relationship with Hoyt and the *Post* was distant. His term was most notably marked by violent conflict over the quality of Denver General Hospital and eruption of a policeman-burglar scandal that hurt the city's reputation nationally; the scandal was only resolved when, partially at Hoyt's personal urging, Governor Stephen McNichols ordered a state investigation that indicted many of Denver's serving officers.

In the election of 1963, the *Post* at first supported William W. Grant, Jr., a prominent civic and political leader, as an independent against both Batterton and Democratic auditor Thomas Currigan. The *Post*'s campaign for Grant, whom Hoyt at times likened to Newton, went all-out, and was unsuccessful. Chastened, the newspaper backed Currigan in the finals to beat the scandal-battered Batterton by some 15,000 votes, and again supported the former auditor in 1967 when he won a second term without a runoff. While never close, Currigan's relationships with Hoyt and the *Post* were cordial, and the mayor gave the publisher great credit for intervention with President Lyndon B. Johnson to secure vital funding for the landmark Skyline Urban Renewal project which remade the face of downtown Denver. But after the Grant defeat, Hoyt's personal interest in mayoral politics waned. Currigan's resignation in 1968 to accept a higher paying job with Continental Airlines brought to power his manager of public works, William H. McNichols, Jr., who put a grip on the city throttle as firm as that of Benjamin Stapleton or Robert Speer. McNichols was a good friend of Hoyt's, part of the publisher's gin rummy and dog-track group of confidants. But Hoyt retired in 1970, and the *Post* supported Joe Shoemaker against McNichols in the former's 1971 try for a first elected term. Shoemaker defeated, the newspaper backed McNichols in the runoff against Democrat Dale Tooley. The paper again went against Tooley, by now the district attorney, in 1975 and backed McNichols for his third term in 1979, which he won without a runoff. To complete the record, the *Post* withdrew support from McNichols's seeking a fourth term in 1983, but its candidate, Tooley, was beaten by Federico Peña, who again defeated *Post*-supported Donald Bain in 1987.

During the 1970s and 1980s, after the hands-on Hoyt's departure, *The Denver Post*'s historic relationship with City Hall became much less personal at the editor and publisher level, and never regained the intensity or enthusiasm with which Hoyt and Quigg Newton set out to redraw, not always successfully, postwar political contours. The newspaper, regardless of election endorsements, built effective working friendships with Denver's mayors throughout the period. These helped spark the change in civic attitudes from the core-city focus of a Stapleton to the wide-awake metropolitanism more characteristic of recent years.

V

Probably no other process of a newspaper's editorial page seems more complex to the reading public than its endorsements of candidates for political office. To most newspapers, endorsement is a civic duty tied to a professional responsibility to comment on government. To some of the public, however, particularly to party politicians, endorsements indicate a newspaper's political personality. In the past, when political parties controlled newspapers, the voice of the paper was indeed the voice of the party. In the case of the early *Denver Post* under

Bonfils and Tammen, while there was no formal party tie, the editorial endorsements were extremely personal, and there was no question but that the political sentiments of ownership were the sentiments of the newspaper. As a legacy of the personal journalism era, even today political endorsements by most newspapers remain the jurisdiction of ownership as expressed by the publisher.

However, in post–World War II journalism there was a growing professionalism about the endorsement process which was characteristic of the editorial page introduced by Hoyt in 1946. He insisted that endorsements be the result of extensive investigation, without regard to party or friendship. Some of the philosophy he injected is mirrored in a 1974 editorial written after his retirement: "No party politics," the *Post* said, "is involved in our endorsement."

> The *Post* is an independent newspaper. We owe nothing to either political party. We have supported independents, Democrats, Republicans, based on opinion as to merit and the welfare of the city, state, and nation. . . . An editorial endorsement of a candidate is nothing more nor less than an opinion intended to stimulate public discussion and to give the newspaper's best judgement for its readers to ponder and weigh as they see fit. Our endorsement system is not beyond criticism. And we are not out to make friends. We are seeking improved government of the people, by the people, and for the people, and so far we have not found a better way to express election opinion than the endorsement system.

The manner in which the *Post* was able to hew to its independent line in the post–World War II years may be judged by Tables 1 and 2. In all, in the eleven postwar presidential contests, the *Post* backed six Republicans, four Democrats, and withheld endorsement once. There were eight winners and two losers (for those who think that winning rather than informing is the goal of the endorsement game); four of the endorsees were incumbents. In the fifteen senatorial races, the *Post* endorsed nine Republicans and six Democrats; its endorsed candidates won nine races and lost six. Seven senatorial endorsees

Table 1

POST ENDORSEMENTS FOR PRESIDENT, 1948-1988
(In Boldface)

YEAR	WINNING CANDIDATE	LOSING CANDIDATE
1948	Truman (D)	**Dewey (R)**
1952	**Eisenhower (R)**	Stevenson (D)
1956	**Eisenhower (R)**	Stevenson (D)
1960	**Kennedy (D)**	Nixon (R)
1964	**Johnson (D)**	Goldwater (R)
1968	Nixon (R)	**Humphrey (D)**
1972	**Nixon (R)**	McGovern (R)
1976	**Carter(D)**	Ford (R)
1980	Reagan (R) *	Carter (R) *
1984	**Reagan (R)**	Mondale (D)
1988	**Bush (R)**	Dukakis (D)

No endorsement

Table 2

POST ENDORSEMENTS FOR U.S. SENATOR, 1948-1988
(In Boldface)

YEAR	WINNING CANDIDATE	LOSING CANDIDATE
1948	Johnson (D)	**Nicholson (R)**
1950	**Millikin (R)**	Carroll (D)
1954	Allott (R)	**Carroll (D)**
1956	Carroll (D)	**Thornton (R)**
1960	Allott (R)	**Knous (D)**
1962	Dominick (R)	**Carroll (D)**
1966	**Allott (R)**	Romer (D)
1968	**Dominick (R)**	McNichols, S. (D)
1972	Haskell (D)	**Allott (R)**
1974	**Hart (D)**	Dominick (R)
1978	**Armstrong (R)**	Haskell (D)
1980	**Hart (D)**	Buchanan (R)
1984	**Armstrong (R)**	Dick (D)
1986	**Wirth (D)**	Kramer (R)
1990	**Brown (R)**	Heath (D)

were incumbents. The personal factor in national office endorsements at the *Post* was stronger in the earlier era of editors
and publishers who had formed strong attachments on the
national scene. Bonfils had even offered the editorship to a
retiring Calvin Coolidge, a prospect that calls for a retroactive
professional wince even today. Bonfils's Depression-era successors belabored Roosevelt's New Deal so vehemently, and were so
isolationist in tone, that the paper had the slimmest of links to
the Washington, D.C., establishment as the country came out of
depression into World War II. During and after the war, Hoyt,
a moderate Republican internationalist, forged many Washington ties. In those days, before the arrival of television, the talk
show, and the televised debate, newspaper moguls played bigger
roles in national politics, and Hoyt relished his links to presi-
dents, somewhat with Dwight D. Eisenhower and especially with
Lyndon Johnson, both of whom had extensive Western and
Colorado ties. Johnson was a close friend of the *Post* publisher
and used to bend his ear in midnight phone calls about the
troubles of the republic in Vietnam.

But the *Post,* holding to a tradition of close scrutiny of
national politicians, did not let past endorsements or friendships stand in the way of shifting support as the newspaper
regarded its duty to the public interest. Perhaps the most
notable example was its early call on November 4, 1973, for the
resignation or impeachment of President Richard M. Nixon
when the Watergate revelations were still just simmering. This
was just a year after Nixon had been endorsed by the paper
for reelection and almost a year before he finally resigned. The
New York Times and *Detroit News,* by coincidence, made the same
call on the same weekend, and the resignation editorials received national attention. The *Post*'s mail from affronted readers ran three to one against this suggestion that a president step
down. No other *Post* editorial attracted as much response in the
postwar period. By the end of the Hoyt era at the *Post,* the
tradition of the newspaper's political independence had been
firmly established.

MOBS SWEEP DENVER

POST IS SACKED, CARS ARE DEMOLISHED

TWO YOUTHS KILLED IN SOUTH DENVER RIOT

MAYOR CALLS FOR 2,000 VOLUNTEER POLICEMEN TO RESTORE ORDER THRU CITY

AUTHORITIES ARE HELPLESS IN ORGY OF TERROR THRUOUT SEVEN HOURS

The Circulation of THE DENVER POST Yesterday Was 133,730

WEATHER FORECAST
Generally fair tonight and Saturday, warmer Saturday

DENVER POPULATION
256,369

THE DENVER POST

46 PAGES
3D EDITION

THE BEST NEWSPAPER IN THE U. S. A.
DENVER, FRIDAY, AUGUST 6, 1920

2c by Newsboys
5c on Trains

Tramway Officials Declare Cars Will Be Kept Running—Chief Armstrong and Nine Patrolmen Injured In Melees—Black Jack Jerome Runs Gantlet of Strikers When Detachment of Strikebreakers Arrives From Los Angeles—Firecracker Starts Riot—Barns Stormed

(By BRUCE A. GUSTIN.)

Hell broke loose in Denver Thursday.

Lawless mobs roamed the streets. They shot and beat citizens, policemen, strikebreakers. They wrecked business buildings and attempted to burn carbarns. They overturned and demolished street cars. They defied all the constituted authorities and endangered the lives of thousands of men, women, children. They halted momentarily the breaking of the street car strike. Two men—both rioters—are dead. 'One rioter is fatally wounded.' Seven persons, including two policemen, are seriously hurt. Thirty-two other persons are less seriously injured, after the wildest evening and night in Denver's history.

Mayor Bailey Friday issued a proclamation calling for 2,000 volunteers to serve as special officers.

The police were utterly unable to cope with the orgy of terror staged in the heart of Denver Thursday night.

The fire department, called into action at 9:30 o'clock when the mob stormed The Denver Post, which always has been a 100-per-cent union shop, was unable to lay hose lines. After breaking all the glass in the front of the building, the mob forced its way thru the police and fire lines, entered the building, attempted to wreck the interior and started a fire in the basement.

One unidentified rioter, believed to be named Lloyd, was killed, two were fatally wounded, and another was shot by strikebreakers at 12:45 o'clock Friday morning when the mob tried to storm and set fire to the South division barns. Warned of the approach of the mob which marched down Broadway, drums beating and men *_____, 150 strikebreakers armed to the teeth, took their positions on top of cars and among cars in the yards.*

SO THE PEOPLE MAY KNOW

IF a mob can come into any man's place of business and in violation of every law of the land wantonly destroy thousands of dollars' worth of valuable machinery, furniture and materials, without the slightest reason or justification, then, indeed, has every man's rights been assassinated, law made a sniveling mockery and life itself a ghoulish farce. And yet all of this and more was done in the center of the city and to The Post last evening.

The Post for twenty-five years had fought to help labor secure every just demand it made, and, strange to say, the very union that is now striking saw the first for which The Post drew the sword years ago, but because we differed from them in the present strike—unmindful of all past service—they or their associates and sympathizers unhesitatingly rushed to our building and tried to burn and destroy it, and their only reason for this outrageous and unjustifiable act is that The Post does not agree with them.

By the bludgeon and torch they seek now

We do not ask you to feel sorry for The Post, nor for its partial destruction, for all material loss can soon be replaced, but we do ask you to feel sorry for such conditions as would make such crimes as this possible anywhere in the United States.

It means that Bolshevism, Sovietism and Anarchy, with gun and torch, have leaped from bloody and ravished Russia to our beloved land. It means that what has happened to The Post may next happen to you. It means that Revolution and its red ring and bloodstained sword, is not a hideous nightmare, but is at the door of every man today.

So do not feel sorry for The Post—feel sorry for yourself, for your children, for your country and for civilization. For no man may know who is next on the list.

The Post remains tranquil and unafraid. It will continue to fearlessly expose wrong and evil by whoever practiced. It will never refuse to be frightened or intimidated by an man or set of men and if the laws of our coun

Front page, August 6, 1920

Special Aerial Picture Coverage on Flood-Ravaged Areas

THE DENVER POST FLOOD FINAL

The Voice of the Rocky Mountain Empire*

Vol. 73, No. 320   Denver, Colo.—Climate Capital of the World—Thursday, June 17, 1965   10 Cents, 84 Pages

South Platte Torrent Deals Denver Worst Disaster

Navy Jets Down Pair Of MIGs

SAIGON. South Viet Nam—(AP)—Two U.S. Navy Phantom jets shot down two Communist MIG7 fighters in flames Thursday in a daylight 30 miles south of Hanoi, the North Viet Nam capital.

The clash occurred while the Phantoms from the carrier Midway were flying escort for other U.S. warplanes bombing North Viet Nam targets.

A U.S. spokesman said four Communist jets appeared and turned toward the American planes as if they were going to attack. But apparently they were hit before they had a chance to open fire, he said.

PARACHUTE SEEN

One parachute was seen opening but it was not known what happened to the Communist pilot. The other two MIGs escaped.

The spokesman said the dogfight lasted 28 seconds and that the Phantoms hit the enemy with air-to-air missiles.

It was presumed that the

Prompt Alarms Keep Toll Low

By LEONARD LARSEN
Denver Post Staff Writer

The flooding South Platte River, fed by cloudburst south of Denver, ripped through the metropolitan area late Wednesday in the worst natural disaster of the city's history.

The normally placid South Platte and dry-stream tributaries were turned into half-mile-wide torrents which swept out bridges, flooded thousands of homes, business stores and factories and for a time ripped the capital city.

Fires touched off by electrical shorts ruptured gas lines and ravage tanks burned throughout the night Wednesday and early Thursday along the river as it roared out of its banks, sweeping out at debris into the industrial area and railroad yards in central Denver.

Miraculously—and because police and volunteers labored to warn persons in its path—the Denver area flood took a limited human toll.

One man was found dead in three feet of water in the Globeville area at north Denver—either from a heart attack or drowning—and a handful of victims were reported treated at area hospitals for injuries, shock and exposure.

These were unconfirmed reports, however, as other persons reported missing and possibly killed by the flood waters.

A State Highway Department spokesman said two drivers were believed lost in the raging waters of Plum Creek near Larkspur on Interstate 25, where the road and bridge

Flood Final

As a special service to our readers, most of the news coverage on this disastrous Denver flood will be found in this first section of today's Flood Final. In addition, readers' attention is called to pages 33, 34, 37, 84.

What Caused Platte Flood? Page 2

Front page, June 17, 1965

ISSUES AND IDENTITY
The Voice of the Rocky Mountain Empire

I

The distinguished American historian Francis Parkman, traveling through what was known as the Great American Desert, camped where Cherry Creek joins the South Platte River in August 1846. He at once noted that "the stream, like most of the others which we passed, was dried up with the heat, and we had to dig holes in the sand to find water for ourselves and our horses." This wilderness experience, twelve years before the first gold seekers founded Denver on that spot, and some fifty years before *The Denver Post* was born, capsulizes the city's umbilical tie to the South Platte River and its fickle creeks. From flood to trickle, the Platte has brought this oasis civilization its essential water, whether the users were few or near two million. But, along with Parkman, Coloradans have endured a near-desert climate and an unsteady supply of surface water from the mountains. And they, too, have incessantly sought water through digging holes, whether small wells, long ditches and tunnels, or large reservoirs. Today's metropolitan Denver water holes are collectively called a "system," and *The Denver Post* has persistently cheered its diggers.

When the *Post* was born in 1892, Denver's water supply from the Platte was delivered to 100,000 residents by ditch, water cart, often-contaminated wells, and pipes from small reservoirs, all fed by the Platte below the mountains. Fires fought with buckets, disastrous floods and recurrent droughts, typhoid and other health epidemics from water pollution, and the lack of indoor plumbing and sewers until 1872—all explain Denver and the *Post*'s historic and obsessive desire for clean and ample water.

Denver residents always knew that from the Platte headwaters in the mountains the snowmelt water would be plentiful if it could be stored for use before it ran off onto the plains. But mountain storage was beyond the means of any of the early water companies. Not until the strongest of the Denver entrepreneurs consolidated the private-monopoly Denver Union Water Company in 1894 did the city's dream of mountain water make economic sense. The company built Cheesman Reservoir above Deckers in 1905, and when this was sold to the city in 1918, the vision that only mountain storage could give Denver a safe water supply became the city government's consistent goal.

The *Post* fulminated against private ownership of the water system and campaigned for public control. When the water company's request for a franchise extension was defeated in 1914, the paper's headline took a joyful tone: "WHOOPEE, PEOPLE WIN." Said the front-page editorial, "In the defeat of the water company yesterday, Denver advanced twenty years, and every interest—real, physical, and moral—increased 100 per cent. . . . It makes every man proud of the name American!"

Denver's water system was built in the following years through persistent efforts to obtain legal water rights and to build facilities to put them to use, as required by law and in the face of an ever-growing population. Drought periods regularly produced public thirst for bond issues and for the aggressive legal and political water entrepreneurship of Denver's water board. Over the years, the system, built without taxes from municipal water sales, included major water-hole reservoirs (Cheesman, 1905; Antero, 1924; Eleven-Mile, 1932; Ralston, 1937; Gross, 1954; and Dillon, 1964); tunnels through the mountains (Moffat, 1937; Williams Fork, 1940; Gumlick, 1940; Vasquez, 1958; and Roberts, 1964); and treatment plants to ensure public health (Kassler, 1890; Marston, 1925; Moffat, 1937; and Foothills, 1983). Cherry Creek Reservoir and Chatfield Dam were added by the federal government to prevent disastrous floods which racked Denver in 1864, 1875, 1912, 1933, and 1965.

Each of these water projects ignited public debate and gained public financing and legal approval only through political persistence (including almost constant support from the *Post,* which for many years gave water supply an editorial priority). Of all these water issues, the thorniest was transmountain diversion, vehemently opposed by Western Slope residents politically and by many taxpayers financially.

Why bother about water across the mountains? Of the two major rivers nearest to Denver, the eastward-running Platte carries only 10 percent of the state's mountain snowmelt, while the Colorado River, just across the Continental Divide, sends 70 percent toward California. Most of the water has always flowed away from the center of greatest population in Colorado, producing the state's toughest political puzzle. As population grew, Denver's purchase of the legal rights to water across the mountains began in the 1920s. Of the total municipal projects to bring Colorado River water to Denver, the largest and most visible was that which backs up Blue River water in Dillon Reservoir and through the Roberts Tunnel under the Great Divide to the Platte and Denver. The long-delayed Two Forks Reservoir was to have offered major downstream storage in this system, allowing greater use of Blue River water while stabilizing Lake Dillon and assuring supply to the Western Slope. When state courts in 1954 refused to give Denver the desired legal priority to this water, the *Post* said, "No city of Denver's size has suffered a more staggering blow from any court action."

In 1955, after several years of drought, 93 percent of Denver's voters supported a $100 million bond issue to improve the water system; later that year the federal government, stimulated by Denver's patron saint Dwight Eisenhower, politically engineered the legal settlement that allowed Denver to use most of its Blue River water if it assured replacement for the Western Slope. When the Blue River system was physically engineered and in place by 1964, it doubled the water that Denver had available for the tremendous post–World War II growth of the metro area, allowing major allocations to the suburbs. It also provided the attractive recreational area of Lake Dillon, then feared but now revered as a solid addition to the Colorado environment.

When Francis Parkman sank the first Anglo water hole recorded on the site of Denver, he wrote a prologue to an amazing story of political, financial, legal—and not a little editorial—toil. To create a metropolis out of wilderness through a clean and ample water supply has been no mean feat. The *Post* wrote in 1959, "Denver is an expanding and bustling community whose continued growth and prosperity are assured—provided only that the city can develop a water supply adequate for the people and industries that will be coming our way in the future." But are we as determined today, as was Parkman in 1846, to dig the water holes that are the lifeblood of modern Denver?

II

In 1991, when Denver inaugurated its first black mayor, Wellington Webb, and toasted his Hispanic predecessor, Federico Peña, it may have been easy to forget the sometimes violent and often abrasive racial competition that was dominant news in *The Denver Post*'s first hundred years. The city and its newspaper had only painfully progressed toward a solid multicultural society that eased its ethnic tension by political rather than violent means, as exemplified in the 1864 Sand Creek Massacre. Before World War II, the paternalistic Anglo dominance of this Colorado city and state was alternately charitable and repressive. There were such spasmodic scars as bitter labor wars with an ethnic fuse, the election of a Ku Klux Klan senator and governor, Depression-era harassment of Hispanic field workers, occasional outbursts of anti-Semitism, and a general tendency on the part of the older establishment to link civil rights activism to the Bolshevik Revolution.

In 1912, Hosokawa reports, the *Post* thought nothing of placing a caption beneath a picture of black heavyweight champion Jack Johnson and his new white bride that said: "The above is a photograph of the culminating outrage of the Twentieth Century. It marks the wreck of our boasted civilization . . . [and] brings the blush of shame to the cheek of every right-thinking American." Hosokawa contrasts this to the story of George Brown, hired as the *Post*'s first black reporter four decades later

in 1950. By 1956 he was a newsroom stalwart and was later
elected, with the newspaper's blessing, as a state senator, point-
ing him toward becoming the state's lieutenant governor in
1974. Palmer Hoyt had introduced news and editorial page
coverage of Denver's minorities and had hired, among others,
Brown and the Nisei journalists Hosokawa and drama critic
Larry Tajiri—all this in the 1950s, well before such minority
hiring became a national newspaper concern.

In 1957, when Governor Orval Faubus of Arkansas ordered
the National Guard to bar nine black students from Little Rock's
Central High School, the *Post* took a strong pro-integration stand,
and six years later sent Brown and John Rogers, a Mississippi-born
white journalist who was later *Post* managing editor, to cover
Martin Luther King's crusade against southern bigotry in Mont-
gomery, Alabama. The National Conference of Christians and
Jews honored the newspaper for its Alabama coverage.

Meanwhile the newspaper had been persistently editorializ-
ing against unfair educational opportunity for minority students
in the Denver schools, which were allowing segregation by neighborhood. The *Post* was also campaigning for fair housing laws
which would break up the ghetto mentality of the Denver real
estate industry and assist in school integration. Shortly after
King was assassinated in 1968, Rachel Noel, the first black
school board member, and board colleague A. Edgar Benton
began the long march by getting the board to authorize its own
mandatory busing-for-integration program. The *Post* editorialized, "There are too many children who are dying, educationally,
everyday in the segregated schools of Denver."

But school integration was not popular in the Denver of that
day. The pro-busing majority on the board was promptly turned
out of office at the next election, and its busing program was
scuttled. So the integrationists, led by pro-bono Holland & Hart
attorney Gordon Griener, then won a substantial victory from
federal judge William Doyle, who was upheld in 1973 by no less
than the U.S. Supreme Court. It ruled that the Denver Public
Schools had purposely gerrymandered a district for "segregative
purpose" and that unless the school board could validate its
action, Denver should "desegregate the entire system, 'root and

branch.'" There followed wide–scale busing between paired schools into the 1990s, which marked the Denver system as one of the most successfully integrated in the country.

Through all of this maneuvering, and during the many school board and municipal elections that revolved on the busing theme, the *Post* consistently supported pro-integration candidates, sometimes winning, sometimes losing. In a 1969 editorial, when two anti-busing members had been elected to the board against the newspaper's solemn advice, an editorial said, "This vote cannot but be seen by many minority people as a rebuff to their aspirations for equality of opportunity in education." In the next few elections, *Post*-backed pro-busing, pro-integration candidates were defeated, but in 1973 and 1975 strong pro-busing candidates won, and by 1976 the newspaper stated: "The full-time pairing of more than 40 Denver elementary schools that started this fall under a federal court desegregation order has proceeded smoothly, thanks to the efforts of largely unsung men and women. They are the monitors appointed by the Community Education Council with the approval of the Federal District Court."

Among the many school board candidates backed by the *Post* in these years, some victorious, some defeated, were Benton, Monte Pascoe, Warren Alexander, Vivian Dodds, Jim Voorhees, David Sandoval, Omar Blair, Bernie Valdez, Katherine Schomp, Larry McClain, Virginia Rockwell, Rev. Marion Hammond, Robert Crider, Fernie Baca-Moore, Carolyn Etter, Carol McCotter, Dorothy Gottleib, Lois Court, Sharon Bailey, Marcia Johnson, and Richard Castro. They, with many others, carried the banner for racially integrated schools in the nation-watched Denver battle. By 1979 the decade-long struggle was mostly over, though with critics contending that busing had caused a debilitating white population flight from Denver's core. The *Post* then editorialized that the "board's burdens have been heavy, trying to cope with declining enrollments, court-ordered busing, shifting neighborhood patterns and changing demands on the school system in a period of budgetary stringency. But as a recent City Council resolution notes, the schools have not only coped, they have overcome."

Not quite. Considering the political controversies of the 1980s about busing, bilingual education, differences between teachers and administration over the labor contract, and disengaging the federal court from control of the school system, the struggle to reduce racism in public education was far from over. But it did mirror remarkable shifts in the attitude of both city government and the *Post* in the course of an embattled century.

III

The Denver Post has always believed it possible to both promote and preserve the wilderness assets of the Rocky Mountains. And until the 1970s that goal of balancing economic development with preservation, a major theme in the newspaper's editorial policy for many years, did not provoke serious opposition. There seemed enough neighborly mountain for every need of a growing city, whether it be clean water supply, ample resource extraction, bountiful tourism and recreation, or readily available spiritual privacy. Bonfils, as the *Post*'s most dominant early editor, was both a development "booster" and an avid fly fisherman, a psychological duality that modern environmental purists have labeled schizophrenia in his successors. He was also an ardent amateur naturalist, which was about as environmentally conscious as any tycoon might be at the turn of the century.

Yet Bonfils indulged flashy stimulations of mountain tourism that would today cast him into the Sierra Club's demonology. As Fowler wrote in *Timber Line:*

> The *Post* fostered a yearly pilgrimage to the Mount of the Holy Cross in Colorado. This peak, containing a cruciform crevice filled with snow, . . . was almost inaccessible until the *Post* campaigned for a road and got in on the ground floor with a summer camp at the base of the sacred hill. Bon' grew very pious about the camp, ballyhooed its beauties and chronicled many miraculous cures that occurred when pilgrims gazed on the natural cross. . . . There were cooks, saddle horses, guides, an orchestra, post-office, lecturers and trails where the young could vary their religious routine with moments of love.

The Bonfils *Post* always stood for "diversity" in the wilderness experience. Fowler recalls Al Birch, the patron saint of *Post* press agents. "To glorify the beauties of [Rocky Mountain] National Park, . . . Mr. Birch publicized it as a Garden of Eden. This phrase suggested a need for an Eve [who could] . . . outdo Robinson Crusoe" and for a month "subsist on roots, berries, and herbs." So Birch recruited an Eve. "On the appointed day [she] arrived at the cabin of Enos Mills, the renowned naturalist, where she changed from civilized garb to the hide of a defunct leopard. She certainly looked fine as she let down her corn-colored hair and stood before the cameras." She was then spirited to a backwoods cabin, and Birch returned to Denver to field many national inquiries. The noble experiment collapsed, however, when after enthusiastic *Post* coverage, an equally enthusiastic Adam showed up at the park to find Eve, who promptly was hustled back to town.

Unfortunately, as the years went on, the fun went out of covering the wilderness scene. The *Post* had a typically Western attitude of ownership of the Rockies and undoubtedly was chagrined when Bernard De Voto, the famous Western historian and author, told the newspaper in a 1950 letter:

> The National Parks and Monuments happen not to be our scenery. They do not belong to Colorado or to the West, they belong to the people of the United States, including the miserable unfortunates who have to live east of the Allegheny hillocks. . . . Don't shoot those unfortunates too loudly or obnoxiously. You might make them so mad that they would stop paying for your water developments.

Actually the *Post* has been a good friend of the federal landlords of the Rockies. The paper strongly supported the first Wilderness Bill in the mid-1960s, and subsequent additions, and had one of the first environmental reporters in the nation, Dick Prouty. But the old conservation idea of balanced use of the mountains remained, as on December 14, 1979, when the paper praised Colorado legislators for cutting back a Carter-era wilderness expansion. The paper feared it would "run roughshod over the interests of many Colorado communities in timbering and rangeland improvement projects. . . . We hope that the resolution also puts an end to the unfair practice of national news media to characterize any non-wilderness forest land as being 'returned to commercial exploitation.'" Later the newspaper noted that "the wilderness lobbies still try to run the nation's huge multiple-purpose natural reserves as if they were a private playpen for environmentalism."

The environmental movement gave the *Post* a real shellacking over the attempt to bring the Winter Olympics to Colorado in 1976. The newspaper had always believed that the winter games would be a great boon to Colorado, developing facilities for winter sports that were bound to arrive anyway, as indeed they did:

> It is ridiculous to accept the gloomy defeatism of Denver Democrats [who included a young representative, Richard Lamm]. . . . Problems of proper land use will be with us whether we hold the Olympics or not. By properly financing the Olympics and by using it as a demonstration that we can guide Colorado's environmental development, our chances of survival will be very, very much improved. It is uncontrolled development—not the Olympic Games—which is the real enemy.

Just before the voters finally turned down public funding for the Olympics by a two-to-one margin in November 1972, propelling Lamm to the governorship two years later, the *Post* said: "This state is clearly going to continue growing in population, Olympics or no Olympics, and the question becomes one of controlling that growth. If we can't control the impact of the Olympics, it is not likely we can control the other types of growth, either."

IV

Two transportation technologies born after the *Post*'s founding have changed profoundly both the newspaper and its Western region. The first local automobile, a Columbia Runabout electric, arrived in Denver in pieces to be assembled in 1899; the first airplane, a Farman biplane, came by boxcar in 1910. Today a Denver without cars, trucks, or airplanes takes some imagination, as does a region without such fruits of internal combustion as suburban living, paved roads, airports, the mountain recreation industry, tourism, global markets, and lifestyles fleeing the Victorian.

In 1900 there were no registered cars in Denver County to surprise a population of 133,859. In 1990, 375,015 cars carried a population of 506,000—the numbers, of course, expanding several times over for the larger metropolitan region. Newspaper automobile advertisements and news coverage were largely responsible for that growth. From the May 1, 1900, advertisements for a $750 Locomobile ("no noise, odor, or vibration") to today's colorful auto sections, the *Post* has been a steady matchmaker for the Westerner loving the command that car or truck gives over Western space. The car's impact on society, for good or bad, was the most constant news story of the *Post*'s century, although not always perceived as such. Stories on improved roads, auto parks, motels, service drive-ins, mountain parks and ski slopes, highway legislation, drunk drivers, air pollution, roving criminals, parking lots, shopping malls, traffic congestion, even mobile sex, were all about "automobility," as historians Leonard and Noel call the phenomenon.

"What a revolution the automobile has brought about in all our ways of life and in all our thoughts," editorialized the *Post* in 1916, vaguely anticipating the change of Denver from a streetcar and railroad city to a fifty-mile-wide automobile metropolis. "It has completely altered the relation of town and country . . . making the farming districts suburbs of our cities." The most metropolitanizing influence on Denver was the freeway system, which began to be planned in the 1930s and developed in the 1940s. The first link was West Sixth Avenue from south of the city center to the World War II Denver Ordnance Plant, now the Federal Center; then came the Denver-Boulder Turnpike in 1952 and the first interstate, I-25, "the Valley Highway," in 1958. But from these beginnings, few planners could foresee how the interstates would create economic, residential, and recreation corridors centered on Denver, forming an arc from Santa Fe, New Mexico, north to Yellowstone Park and from the Great Plains states west to Utah.

Originally, as with the railroads and later the air routes, Denver's transcontinental highway dreams seemed dashed by the rugged central Rocky Mountains; the lower and easier routes for transportation engineers have always been through southern Wyoming or central New Mexico. Denver and its representative paper had to hard sell the economic truth that the Front Range Rockies are not a barrier but a beacon, and that for highways, new tunnels were the answer as they had been for water and rails. As Colorado struggled to be included in east-west interstate planning, the *Post* editorialized: "It is time for members [of the legislature] to awake to what they will be doing to Colorado if they fail to pass a highway tunnel bill. . . . The omission of Colorado from the east-west interstate system is unfair to this state [and] it does not make sense, from a strategic standpoint, to ignore the route which might be the safest and least vulnerable in the event of war." (The interstate system had been partly conceived as essential to defense in the Cold War era.)

Eventually Denver's persistent optimism about transportation—and such leaders as Senator Gordon Allott, Governor Edwin "Big Ed" Johnson, Denver Mayor William Nicholson, Sr., and many others—sold Denver's favorite son-in-law, Dwight Eisenhower, on building I-70 through the Colorado Front Range. The president added three hundred Colorado miles to I-70 and approved the Eisenhower and Johnson Continental Divide tunnels, enabling such meccas to match our mountains as Summit County, Vail, Aspen, and the Grand Junction area.

The development of Denver as a major commercial aviation center, and the *Post*'s stories and editorials thereon, had many strains similar to the highway situation—mushrooming numbers of aircraft with their remarkable shrinking of the wide open Western spaces, developing municipal airport industries, growing federal regulation and finance, and the constant need to recall that the Rockies need not bar Denver from airways anymore than they had from railroads, highways, or water supply. Small plane aviation grew rapidly from the first such flight in

1911, and by 1918 the federal government decided to develop a transcontinental air mail route, which passed through Cheyenne to avoid the Rockies. By 1926 Denver had a feeder mail route to connect with the main line at Pueblo, and various small airfields grew up in the counties, one in Adams County being named for Charles Lindbergh, whose flight to Paris stimulated major Denver demand for commercial passenger air service.

Mayor Benjamin Stapleton was determined to construct a municipal airport, and after much debate among six possible sites, present Stapleton Airport was selected because of its isolated location distant from developed areas. There were many challenges to the city's authority to go into the airport business, and the *Post* called the site "Stapleton's Folly" and "Simpleton's Sand Dunes." But by October 1929, when the airport was dedicated a few weeks before the great stock market crash, the newspaper was singing its praises. The airport suffered some rocky first years during the Depression, but by 1934 small commercial carriers had taken over the government mail service, and by 1937 its first trunk passenger carriers, United and Continental, were in place.

From that point on, the modernization of the airport continued steadily though always with controversy, and Stapleton International Airport became a major hub in the nation, serving well until the 1990s, when runway and neighborhood safety problems for ever-enlarging aircraft and capacity requirements for international air routes motivated a shift, amid the usual acrimony. The new international airport at $3 billion would have the same first tenants as Stapleton at $430,000—United and Continental. Landlocked Denver continues to survive and prosper by being on the cutting edge of transportation technology, and *The Denver Post* continues to hammer on that fact as it has for most of the twentieth century.

V

At the end of World War II, the Daniels and Fisher (D&F) Tower was the dominant spire on downtown Denver's skyline.

Only fifty years ago, there existed no Auraria campus, no Lower Downtown Historic District, no Seventeenth Street or Broadway skyscrapers, no Sixteenth Street Mall, no Larimer Square or Tabor Center, and no convention centers or the Denver Center for the Performing Arts. "Downtown" was substantially the low-profile, brick-and-stone city of the late nineteenth and early twentieth centuries, now glimpsed in such preserved examples as the Masonic, Denver Dry, Kittredge, and Equitable buildings; the warehouse district; and the residences in Ninth Street Historic Park on the Auraria campus. This old downtown was still the retailing core of the region, and the auto-aided exodus to outlying shopping malls and such other competitors as the Denver Tech Center was only a shadow on its bumptious civic horizon.

Despite the perennial complaints that Denver lacks civic leadership, this transformation of an outdated, early-century urban mass into the modern and attractive downtown Denver was a major achievement in city building. It was pushed by several city administrations, various Chamber of Commerce drives, nationally recognized planning efforts, substantial financing from the federal urban renewal program, a determined historic preservation effort, and consistently by the editorial pages of *The Denver Post*.

The *Post* began urging the community to take advantage of the Federal Housing Act (urban renewal) of 1954 almost as soon as it was passed. Basically the federal government would put up two thirds if the city would pay one third of renewal project costs. This formula resulted in the clearing and low-cost sale to developers of twenty-seven blocks in the Skyline Urban Renewal Project, bounded by Cherry Creek, Larimer, Twentieth, and Curtis streets, and of the 169-acre site for the Auraria Higher Education Project. The main engine of this massive change was the Denver Urban Renewal Authority (DURA), established in 1958 and still a key player in downtown's future. After a few smaller projects, DURA hit full stride with Skyline in 1968, a project which took almost two decades to complete. As Leonard and Noel put it, "Normally . . . DURA simply knocked buildings down or blew them up. Preservationists howled, but there was no stopping DURA as it bulldozed the ground for the Tabor Center, Prudential Plaza, Sakura Square, Denver National Bank Plaza, the Denver Center for the Performing Arts, and more than a dozen other major developments."

The Skyline project, as with the other urban renewal efforts, was bitterly and successfully delayed in several city elections by conservative elements that did not want the city to pay its share. The impasse was only decisively broken by the great Platte River flood of June 1964. Flood damage impressed President Lyndon Johnson with the need to do something extra for Denver, and the solution proposed by his close friend Palmer Hoyt was to allow Denver a $26 million credit to the Skyline project for the already built Currigan Convention Center. Johnson pushed through an amendment to housing legislation at the eleventh hour, and Skyline had its significant seed money. A *Post* editorial of July 5, 1966, said: "Thank You, Mr. President . . . . The President was deeply disturbed at the damage inflicted on this city by the great flood of two weeks ago. . . . He understood that the funds that might have been raised for the city's share of Skyline would now have to be used to pay repair bills, and that the project might be held up indefinitely. So the President threw his support behind a special amendment." Denver voters followed through by approving Skyline with a 71 percent margin in May 1967.

As DURA's bulldozers rolled, the alarmed historic preservation community began to organize. The *Post* had originally supported DURA's refusal to accept a preserving landmark designation for ten historic buildings in the project area, and only the prompt entrepreneurialism of preservation developers Dana and John Crawford saved the Larimer Square block. By the time DURA was aiming at the D&F Tower, the newspaper was having second thoughts: "The D&F Tower is not any Taj Mahal or Sacré Couer. . . . [It is] admittedly something only an older Denver could love. Yet that love is involved and deeply so. And when dealing with that passion even the efficient, incorrupt, and progressive politicians and urban developers of 1978 might well stand back, take a second breath and ask themselves if what they are doing is as right as it is legal and 'necessary.'" The D&F Tower was finally saved but only after a court battle, led by the Colorado Historical Society's Stephen Hart, that went to the Tenth U.S. Circuit Court of Appeals. Between 1968 and 1974, DURA also cleaned out Auraria, the city's oldest residential neighborhood, as the site for the new education center. Again a few units were preserved as the Ninth Street Historic Park by the initiative of Historic Denver, Inc., then directed by Barbara Sudler.

Reaction to the clean-sweep policies of DURA, as well as the growing environmental consciousness of the late 1960s and 1970s, is given part credit for the founding of Historic Denver, Inc., and the Denver Landmark Preservation Commission. The *Post* supported gradual increases in the Landmark Commission's few powers, and two major city planning efforts of the 1980s gave further clue to growing support for historic preservation on the part of the city's political and business establishments. The Downtown Plan led to the success of the Lower Downtown Historic District, and the Comprehensive Plan of 1989, unanimously adopted by the administration and city council, gave preservation a higher priority in city policy, a trend summarized in early 1992 when Jennifer T. Moulton, Historic Denver's president, was made the city's first woman planning director.

An example of the changed attitudes came in a *Post* editorial of July 11, 1990, concerning the Central Bank Building, about to be destroyed: "Tragically, this grand old dame didn't have to die. She could have remained a vibrant part of downtown if only four intransigent and insensitive corporations could have reached a common sense agreement. . . . Perhaps someone should erect a sign beside the ugly parking lot that will likely replace the wonderful historic structure, 'This eyesore was brought to you by the following corporations.'" It was a far cry from the days when the paper refused to help save ten historic buildings in the twenty-seven-block Skyline area. Today, as downtown Denver slowly springs back from the late-eighties economic recession and the nationwide restructuring of its retailing patterns, the business and preservation communities have forged new alliances to maintain the momentum that built a new downtown for Denver, with the *Post* still in the thick of the editorial action.

VI

The Denver Post's casting as a regional "voice" stemmed as much from geography, history, and economics as from institutional pride. While today newer technologies have dissolved much of the emptiness and isolation of our wide open spaces, not so long ago the leading metropolitan daily newspaper was much more the dominant communications representative of a region. For example, when the *Post* was born, no cars, airplanes, radios, televisions, films, or daily editions of national publications knit the Mountain West into the national and world web, and only Denver was marked by location and size to be the major city center seeking a national voice.

And there was someone out there in the nation to listen. The "West" at the turn of the century, whether as a "closing" frontier, as a recreational playground or natural resource treasury, as a bubbling stew of adolescent cities, or as the dreamland of myth, literature, and art, was popular in the national dialogue. Such regional fans as President Theodore Roosevelt, William "Buffalo Bill" Cody, Frederic Remington, Charles Russell, and many others, including the *Post*, constantly inserted the West into this national conversation.

To be a regional voice, a daily newspaper needed, first, a reasonable economic strength and size; second, owners, editors, and readers with a commitment to regional concerns; and, third, a distinctive region to cover. Over the years the *Post* has gone through economic ups and downs which affected its regional circulation, and its policies have gone through generational changes of *Post* people whose hearts were into differing aspects of the West. But the newspaper never abandoned its effort to be something special to that arc of oases from Santa Fe and Albuquerque in the south to the northern borderlands of Wyoming, and from the montane valleys of western Colorado to the wheat hamlets of the high plains. From Buffalo Bill Cody, late in his career a *Post* promotion flack, through the revered cowboy-reporter Red Fenwick, to our present-day Rocky Mountain Ranger, Jim Carrier, a long line of *Denver Post* Western enthusiasts negotiated a generous portion of news space for regional coverage. They were continuing the priorities set by Tammen and Bonfils, including such flamboyant promotions as the historic Cheyenne Frontier Days special train, Wild West shows, and mountain festivals of which today's Ride to the Rockies is a vigorous successor.

As an outstanding example of this century of concern for region as well as city, state, and nation, consider *Empire,* the Sunday magazine of *The Denver Post.* It became one of the nation's most successful newspaper magazines in thirty-seven years of publication, from 1949 to 1986. As to the concept of *Empire, Post* editor and publisher Palmer Hoyt in 1946 adopted the slogan "Voice of the Rocky Mountain Empire" and maintained that "this is an empire in fact, united in history, character, climate, community interest, and ambition. And *The Denver Post* should perforce be its voice—there is no other metropolitan newspaper which even attempts to serve the entire region."

The *Post* had long published feature sections and pages in rotogravure, the slick-paper printing process that gave newspapers their first high quality graphics. After World War II, the paper's tepid *Weekly Magazine* section was upgraded, and after 1950 when the *Post* moved into a new California Street plant with its own "roto" presses, *Empire* became a stand-alone magazine with its own editorial and advertising staffs, commanding a substantial share of the newspaper's purse. *Post* historian Hosokawa, the longtime *Empire* editor and backbone, states that "*Empire* . . . set out to make itself the dominant magazine in its circulation area. This was no pipe dream because, being distributed with the Sunday *Post,* it went into many more homes in the area than national publications like *Reader's Digest, Life, Saturday Evening Post,* and all the others." Bernard Kelly, long assistant editor of *Empire,* once heard an expert urge newspaper magazines to concentrate on women readers and their four F's—food, fashion, furniture, and family. This was definitely not the *Empire* approach, which featured magazine-quality writing and photography on all regular topics of news coverage, but with a regional angle.

Some of the more interesting *Empire* features recalled by Hosokawa include Bill Barker's saga of Bridey Murphy, a 1954 Pueblo housewife whose previous life in early nineteenth-century Ireland was resurrected by hypnotists Morey Bernstein and Bill Thomson; Jack Guinn's 1966 award-winning series on the last Indian wars from the native viewpoint; Cary Stiff's series on blacks in the early West, which stimulated the first academic studies in that subject; Red Fenwick's and Jack Kisling's perennial columns on hometown folks of the West, including Chauncey and Clyde Smaldone, Denver Prohibition entrepreneurs; Olga Curtis's study of "Sex and the Single Teenager" in 1963, before the topic was commonplace; the first four-color photographs of men walking on the moon, beating *Life* magazine into print; and numerous quality graphics from artists H. Ray Baker and Joe Barros. "These were the exceptional features," Hosokawa writes, "but week after week *Empire*'s stock-in-trade was interesting stories from the far reaches of the Rocky Mountain Empire. Writer Zeke Scher and photographer George Crouter teamed up to specialize in fascinating material from distant places. . . . Indefatigably they took *Empire* readers over rarely traversed trails to mountain heights and canyon depths not often seen."

This regional formula proved good newspaper economics, for a while. By the mid-1970s, Hosokawa states, "*Empire* was second only to the New York *Times Magazine* in total advertising, with such giants as the Chicago *Tribune* and Los Angeles *Times* magazines trailing . . . [and] in 1973 . . . *Empire* won the *Editor & Publisher* magazine's first prize for creative use of editorial color in newspaper magazines." This success, as a side effect, pushed the *Post* into the rotogravure printing business; its subsidiary, Gravure West Corporation in Los Angeles, and the Denver plant at their peak published newspaper magazines for the *Kansas City Star, Seattle Times, Oklahoma City Oklahoman, San Jose Mercury News,* and the *Los Angeles Herald Examiner,* the whole process being a major contribution to *Post* history of business manager and later chief executive Charles R. Buxton.

Alas, for old *Empire* buffs, new offset printing methods which improved color in regular sections of newspapers began to lure advertising away from rotogravure supplements in the 1980s. In addition, escalating costs, a retail recession, and the newer printing presses and processes brought to the *Post* by its modernizing Times Mirror and MediaNews ownerships, made an end to *Post* rotogravure printing and to *Empire* magazine inevitable. But its memory lingers as a milestone in the newspaper's continuing role as the "Voice of the Rocky Mountain Empire."

VII

The overriding news story of the *Post*'s first hundred years was the emergence of the United States as an international power, even though the vast and empty Mountain West had never been as isolated from global influences as its more romantic fans liked to remember. After all, Colorado became "American" in one of the biggest international real estate deals of all time, the Louisiana Purchase, and its fur, mining, cattle, and farming economies over the years were integrally, if often invisibly, linked to foreign financial control. But at about the time the paper was coming into its own, the Spanish-American War of 1898 and the First World War of 1914–18 cast both nation and region into a world role which they never again could escape, even in the empty spaces of the Wild West. "Entanglements" to the isolationists, "responsibilities" to the internationalists, these world linkages changed the face of the news; no longer could the *Post* live by its founders' dictum that dogfights on Champa Street were of more interest to readers than famines in Timbuktu.

Taken broadly, the *Post*'s first half century until the 1940s was one of editorial disinterest in foreign involvement, of fear of the "Red menace" created by the Russian Revolution of 1917, and of suspicion, veiled and unveiled, toward the immigration that world change delivered to Denver. This more-or-less isolationist stance did not shift until World War II, the great catalyst that converted the majority of the nation and its regional newspaper

voices to a more worldly focus. On both its news and opinion
pages, the postwar *Post* gave vigorous coverage and support to
the Marshall Plan for European revival; to the growth of the
NATO alliance; to American involvement in the Korean War; to
the political and military "containment" of the Stalinist Soviet
Union; to the watershed presidential election of Denver's favorite internationalist son-in-law, Dwight D. Eisenhower; to the
many foreign aid interventions abroad, such as the Peace Corps
and food shipments to distressed areas; to the United Nations;
and to such early communications forays across the Iron Curtain
as Radio Free Europe and the Voice of America.

To get closer to the national and international issues, the *Post*
in 1946 established a Washington bureau reporting to Hoyt, and
staffers covered various stories around the globe. With at one
time the second largest "news hole," or dedicated copy space, of
any afternoon paper in the country, the *Post* subscribed to more
news services than any paper in the region, printed the full texts
of presidential press conferences, and participated heavily in the
public policy and training sessions of professional press organizations. International coverage was mandated in the front
sections of the enlarged paper. Major national and international
stories of the Hoyt era (1947–70) to which the *Post* gave extensive staff coverage included attacks by isolationist Senator Joseph McCarthy on supposed Communist penetration of the
State Department; the nation's wars against communism, hot in
Asia and cold elsewhere; the assassination of John F. Kennedy;
and the space race with the USSR leading to the world's first
lunar landing.

Perhaps the finest hour for Hoyt's *Post* in the eyes of
professional journalists was its early and relentless scrutiny of
McCarthy and his guilty-until-proven-innocent inquisition
against presumed Communists in the federal government. Hoyt
laid down guidelines for the *Post*'s staff regarding McCarthy's
charges against government servants—always to evaluate the
source of the charge, to play the stories as they would if they
were not coming from a senator with immunity, to withhold
publication of charges until the answers of the accused could be
included, and to avoid color in favor of fact in headlines on

McCarthy stories. For this doughty opposition to McCarthy, the University of Arizona gave Hoyt its first John Peter Zenger Freedom of the Press Award in 1954, because he had "simultaneously fought to safeguard due process and individual constitutional rights [with] the fight to protect the community from infiltration by subversives—*The Denver Post* has fought for both safeguards as essential to survival of the free American way of life."

The McCarthy hearings, which led to Senate ethical condemnation of the senator's activity, were the first such brought by television into America's homes, hitherto the news domain of newspapers and radio. Ten years later, the nation's growing involvement in Vietnam and the space race with the Soviets were being all but smothered by the television tube, to the intense interest of *Post* readers living amid major defense and space establishments. The *Post* was at first skeptical about sending American troops again to the Asian mainland, but by 1964 it agreed with the vast majority in American polls that "if we lost South Vietnam the odds are we'll lose several more rounds—Cambodia, Thailand, Burma by default, and still have to fight again in some place like Malaysia or India or Korea, or else see the Chinese Communists take over all of mainland Asia. This is what the fight is all about. These are the stakes." Hoyt's intimate, midnight-phone-call relationship with President Johnson and visits to Vietnam by *Post* correspondents helped keep the newspaper alert to the progress of the war, and of the effort to build up South Vietnam's strength. Interesting supplements were several editorial briefings by Col. John Paul Vann, on leave from his advisory role in Vietnam to his Colorado residence. Vann, before dying in Vietnam, was to lose faith in the effort, as told in Neil Sheehan's *A Bright Shining Lie,* but during his *Post* visits he conveyed a sincere enthusiasm that the South Vietnamese government could pull itself together. However, President Johnson left office in 1969, Hoyt retired in 1970, Vann died with his boots on, and a new set of politicians, soldiers, and editors faced the deluge.

The drain on the American conscience of the Vietnam experience was partially offset by the successes in the space race, including the walk on the moon, July 20, 1969. The *Post* had made a specialty of the space race, since some of the astronauts were lifted by Denver-built Titan missiles; the whole bevy of satellites was monitored by the North American Air (later Aerospace) Defense Command in Colorado Springs; and several of the astronauts were Colorado citizens. As a result, space became a prime *Post* beat, and the late Dan Partner, one of the nation's premier space reporters, covered launchings at Cape Canaveral and the space-monitoring center in Houston as thoroughly as he would have City Hall. The *Post* was becoming a major source of national and international news, because its Western region was ever more closely tied to the world system of politics, finance, and communication. It was a long path from the Spanish-American War of 1898 to the Gulf War of 1990, including a stop on the moon, but the *Post* symbolically made the whole trip.

Front page, March 8, 1935

Front page, May 21, 1927

Denver Post *city room, mid–1970s*

CRISIS AND STABILITY
Toward a New Century

I

From 1960 until 1972, *The Denver Post*'s management and workers waged bitter warfare against newspaper magnate Samuel I. Newhouse as he attempted to buy control of the paper. The extensive litigation, expense, and draining of energy necessary to thus protect the *Post*'s local ownership may now seem unremarkable to the public after three decades of such newspaper takeovers, but the battle dominated the newspaper in that crucial era. When the *Post* began economic and editorial renovation at the end of World War II, four out of five American daily newspapers were locally owned. However, the next fifty years brought increasing costs, declining dividends, and fragmenting motives among family owners. By 1990, in an almost exact reversal of that percentage, four out of five papers were in non-local group ownership, the *Post* among them.

To the newspaper generation represented by *Post* president Helen G. Bonfils and editor and publisher Palmer Hoyt, local ownership was incontestably vital to the building of a city and a region. Helen Bonfils was proudly determined to maintain the link between her father's paper and the city of Denver which had endured since 1895, and Hoyt hated group-ownership journalism. To their mind-set, Newhouse was a symbol of all that was wrong. He had been adding properties to his newspaper group since the 1930s, and his labor and editorial policies were anathema to many workers at the *Post*. Newhouse believed every paper had its price. Thus he had no particular reason to think in 1960, when he bought 15 percent of *The Denver Post*'s stock from Helen's estranged sister, May Bonfils Stanton, that he was taking a tiger by the tail. But he never got another *Post* share, thanks to Helen Bonfils and an alert, if embattled, *Post* management.

Why did May Bonfils Stanton sell to Newhouse? There had been years of family bitterness which had left her outside the center of *Post* control and at odds with Helen. And the stream of dividends which supported her generous lifestyle and philanthropies had begun drying up as the postwar *Post* plowed more money into modernization. May Bonfils received an average of $212,000 a year in dividends from 1935—when her father's estate was settled—until 1949 but only an average of $80,314 from that time until she sold. Similar revenue withering was irritating the trusts and heirs to the Tammen half of the paper; thus when Newhouse bought his minority interest, he found some Denver financiers sympathetic to his charges of *Post* mismanagement and cool to Hoyt's expensive vision of "empire."

The takeover war that followed was bitter and stretched out, with the outcome in doubt until the last legal battle. It cost Helen Bonfils some $10 million personally in addition to large numbers of *Post* shares. And it deflected top *Post* executives from single-mindedly focusing on the newspaper's improvement at a time when rivals in both print and electronic journalism, including the *Rocky Mountain News,* were gaining circulation and advertising market share. In addition to regular newspapering in an event-packed era, *Post* managers were coping with creating a stock purchase plan aimed at eventual employee ownership, buying stock to steer it away from Newhouse and toward employees, and deferring some management decisions to the non-newspapering necessities of a stream of lawsuits and lawyers.

The Denver Post Employee Stock Trust was roughly modeled after that of the *Milwaukee Journal,* which achieved an employee ownership that still exists. This had long been a dream of Hoyt's but became more than a dream when Miss Helen, without family successors, adopted it as the vehicle to foil Newhouse, guarantee perpetual local ownership, and reward employees for many of whom she displayed deep affection. Though Miss Helen had spent most of her middle years as a professional New York actress and producer, leaving detailed management of the *Post* to others, she kept an eagle eye on the *Post*'s business and employee affairs, and on the paper's role in the community. And she had learned from her father's mercurial career to know a newspaper war when she saw one. Thus, when Newhouse attacked, she called in New York attorney Donald R. Seawell as her confidant and major-domo in the legal battles ahead. From her personal holdings she gave substantial stock to the Employee Stock Trust inventory so that employees could buy shares at half price. She later established a foundation for all her *Post* stock for sale only to the employee trust. The key idea was that employees bought shares which they had to sell back upon death or retirement; thus they would profit from the paper's growth, but the trust would hold the stock permanently, guaranteeing local control.

This plan was on the legal workbench, to minority stockholder Newhouse's vigorous objection, when *Post* management had its chance to buy a first bloc of stock that had been left in trust to Children's Hospital by Tammen. The *Post* picked up this stock just two days before Newhouse made a competing and higher offer, as with the next bloc held for Tammen heirs. Both of these stock purchases by the *Post* were contested in litigation, first by the Tammen heirs and then by Newhouse directly, on the grounds that the stock must be sold to the highest bidder no matter what, and that the employee stock plan was not a proper management goal but just a subterfuge to block Newhouse. In the first court ruling, the *Post* was allowed to keep the purchased shares but Miss Helen was made to pay a surcharge to bring the price up to what Newhouse might have offered. In a second suit, the district court, to the *Post*'s dismay, ordered that all the stock purchased had to go on public sale, and it looked as if Newhouse might finally prevail.

However, a *Post* legal team headed by former U.S. Supreme Court Justice Arthur Goldberg went to the Tenth U.S. Circuit Court of Appeals, which on December 29, 1972—a dozen years after Newhouse had shot his way into town—gave the *Post* its "victory" for local ownership. The court ruled, in dismissing all

Newhouse charges, that both the employee stock purchase plan and the quest to guarantee local ownership were legitimate management options for the *Post*, regardless of their effect on profits. The long fight was over, and Newhouse sold back his stock a few years later, at a profit of $1.2 million. The Bonfils foundations emerged with 91 percent of *The Denver Post*'s ownership, and the employee trust with about 9 percent. But by this time Helen Bonfils was dead, Hoyt had retired, and the road they had charted toward perpetual local ownership of the newspaper looked nowhere near as smooth as they had dreamed.

II

During the 1970s—as wags had it—the building crane was becoming the Colorado state bird. From 1940 to 1950, firing the post–World War II boiler in Denver, metropolitan population increased from 384,000 to 563,000. The 1950s added 350,000, and then came the real boom. From 1960 to 1980 another 700,000 arrived, from Colorado's towns and villages and from the nation's. The 1970s saw such building projects as the Auraria Higher Education campus, the twenty-plus-block Skyline Urban Renewal Project in downtown Denver, the suburban Denver Tech Center, and foothills real estate.

At the locally owned *Denver Post,* this growth started a constantly more expensive race for the advertising dollar and for more readers against ever-fiercer competition from television and from the *Rocky Mountain News,* both nationally owned and financed. Rising costs of personnel, circulation, newsprint, and depreciating equipment plagued a *Post* top-management already under takeover siege from newspaper magnate Samuel Newhouse.

Still the *Post* entered the 1970s with bright hopes for continued prosperity, thinking its ownership was eventually to pass to its employees. When Hoyt retired on December 31, 1970, his *News* counterpart, Jack Foster, retiring in the same year, thought the *Post*'s prospects solid. "With all our sturdy competition," he wrote Hoyt, "we have given to this community two newspapers with its best interests always at heart. I would not want a better competitor than you and *The Denver Post* have been. . . . You can look back and say 'I have made a great newspaper. I have helped make a great community. I have made great young newspapermen to carry on.'"

In carrying on after Hoyt's twenty-four years on the newspaper's bridge, the controlling owner, Helen Bonfils—by now seriously ill—stepped up to chairman; Donald Seawell, her straw boss for the legal fight against Newhouse, became president and chief executive; and Hoyt's right-hand man, Charles R. Buxton, was made the new editor and publisher. Buxton had been operating the paper as Hoyt withdrew and was a like advocate of local control. He engineered a smooth transition, but the *Post* spirit for employee ownership was further shaken when Miss Helen died on June 6, 1972, a few months before the Tenth U.S. Circuit Court of Appeals ruled that the *Post*'s tactics against Newhouse, including the employee ownership plan, had been legitimate, thus ending the takeover threat. As the pressmen "rang the bell" and stopped production in tribute to their departed patron, the *Post* editorialized:

> Some newspaper owners are remote and indistinct figures to the people who work for them and to the communities in which their businesses flourish. This could never be said of Helen G. Bonfils. She was passionately involved with her community and with *The Denver Post*—and in neither case was it an involvement with an abstraction. In plain terms, she loved the people of Denver and the people of the *Post*.

These historic *Post* changes occurred in an era of tumultuous news events which required increasing coverage. In 1969 the *Post* led all afternoon papers in the country in total editorial and news space. This news hole was substantially maintained in the 1970s, and was absorbed, for example, by the Vietnam fiasco; by the Watergate scandal, which led to President Nixon's resignation and replacement by Gerald R. Ford; by the growing environmental movement, including its successful campaign against hosting the Winter Olympics in Colorado; by increasing Hispanic and black civic involvement; by the urban renewal of Denver's downtown; by the "Orange" sports obsession of Denver with its up-and-down Broncos; by Mayor William H. McNichols's progressive administration of city development; and by the glitter of the oil/energy opera, with billionaires Marvin Davis and Philip Anschutz in colorful leading roles. It was a great news decade and the *Post* covered it in a style that many critics found of high quality. As one index of the *Post*'s changing national status, in 1979 editor William H. Hornby was elected president of the American Society of Newspaper Editors, the organization that on ethics complaints had pressured Bonfils out of membership a half century earlier.

In addition to extensive editorial coverage, the *Post* of the 1970s was also investing heavily in rotogravure printing operations; in updating presses and other equipment, including the first newsroom computers; in land for future expansion on its California and Fifteenth Street block; and in substantial improvement of pension plans. This internal investment amounted to some $50 million during the decade. Seawell, as chief executive for fourteen years, attests that during that time "*The Denver Post* never had a losing year. . . . Average annual net profit was in excess of $2 million . . . [and] the final year, 1979, showed a net of $5.2 million at a time when other afternoon papers throughout America were incurring major losses."

If the *Post* was economically stable, why as the 1970s progressed did the directors of its now-governing Bonfils foundations begin to think about selling? Among the reasons:

1. *The Denver Post* Employee Stock Trust was growing at too slow a rate to let it acquire majority ownership, or to be able to raise expansion capital in the foreseeable future. From a start of some 8 percent, the employees had only achieved 18 percent ownership by 1980.

2. While improved, the *Post*'s fifty-year-old presses would obviously not be replaced and thus help the afternoon newspaper make the necessary change to the morning publication field, except by an ownership with substantially more capital.

3. The Bonfils foundations, the majority *Post* owners, were using their capital to build the new Denver Center for the Performing Arts (DCPA). Federal legislation made it necessary for them to either sell their *Post* ownership or to restrict their

outlays to a public entity, such as the DCPA, which they felt to be in keeping with Helen Bonfils's wishes. Later critics claimed that Seawell and the DCPA "bled the *Post* dry," thus making sale inevitable. But the DCPA received only such *Post* funds as were paid out in dividends to any stockholder, including the employee stockholders, and the paper's financial statements to the federal government show that no operating funds were diverted.

By the end of the 1970s, with local newspapers more commonly yielding to group owners, many at the *Post* were beginning to realize that employee ownership was an impossible dream. After many negotiations, some of them with local business leaders such as Davis and Anschutz, *The Denver Post* was sold to the Times Mirror Corporation of Los Angeles for $95 million, effective January 1, 1981. The sale was greeted by *Post* employees with surprising warmth. Times Mirror was Western, its *Los Angeles Times* maintained fraternal standards, and, at least, the new owner was not Samuel Newhouse.

III

When the Times Mirror Corporation took control of the *Post* at the end of 1980 there were some cheers in the newsroom. Though locally owned since 1895, and despite a keen memory of the legal and financial turmoil the paper had endured, local control as a dominating goal was now beyond the newspaper's capital resources. Hence cheers that the *Post* was going to have deep pockets to match those of the rival fast-growing *Rocky Mountain News,* financed by the national Scripps Howard organization and coming on strong in the morning delivery field. Morning publication was more and more conventional wisdom's answer to metro newspaper problems.

Times Mirror did have deep pockets. Its *Los Angeles Times* represented the management "culture" and quality of journalism to which the *Post* aspired, and other prospective purchasers surfacing in the booming Denver economy had less professional agendas. By contrast, in Times Mirror the *Post* got ownership with a presumed special place for the West at heart; Times

Mirror's chief, Otis Chandler, was an old friend of Hoyt's, and this regional link between Denver and Los Angeles promised a real strengthening of Western journalism—or so it seemed to Hoyt's heirs at the paper. Times Mirror had exhaustively studied the *Post* and its formidable problem of being an afternoon delivery paper in one of America's few remaining two-newspaper metropolitan markets. Its owners thought the newspaper worth a solid $95 million since the *Post* had the overall circulation lead in Denver and was turning a modest profit. The Denver economy was still vibrant, and if the *Post*'s antiquated presses could be modernized and some real money put into promotion and distribution, the future looked bright, as it did to other national firms then buying into Denver. One symbol of the surge in sales to national owners was that three Denver business landmarks—the *Post,* the Brown Palace, and the Denver Broncos—all passed from local control in that same year.

What the Times Mirror people could not foresee was the drastic decline in the Mountain West's economy that began in the mid-1980s, coupled with the failure of initial tactics to perform management miracles swiftly. To the surprise of the local management, the new Times Mirror team for the *Post,* headed by publisher Lee J. Guittar, came from the *Dallas Times Herald,* not the *Los Angeles Times;* and although *The Denver Post* staff was ready to swallow new medicine, this was hard to take from a Dallas group that disdained Denver as a community and the *Post*'s older newspaper values. New management brooms swept briskly, and few key players of the old *Post* held their former jobs or responsibilities in a year's time. Bright and promising staffers were imported, but their "culture" was almost certainly not that of the *Los Angeles Times.*

Besides the personnel shuffles, marketing surveys, and experimenting with format that mark any new newspaper administration, the Guittar regime, as it had in Dallas, decided to take the *Post* very quickly into the morning delivery field in head-on competition with the *News.*✠ *Post* readers had been accustomed

✠ Whether the Guittar pace in "going morning" was too hectic or his crew's attitude toward Denver too abrasive depends on one's stance at the time. As the soon-displaced editor of the old *Post,* I had expected the skillful swords of the *Los Angeles Times* and not the bowie knives

to their paper in the afternoon for some seventy years, and the speed of this assault on habit cost the *Post* dearly in circulation and market share at a time when the *News* was pumping its circulation to new heights. "Good Morning Colorado" said the edition of September 14, 1981, announcing for Denver in Guittar's words "a morning newspaper it can be proud of." The decision to "go morning" was no surprise. In the 1970s, management had seen that afternoon metropolitan papers were dying, and that people's reading habits were changing with evening television, single-parent families, and rush-hour traffic that impeded delivery. The lack of capital to fund morning delivery had moved the Bonfils-Tammen ownership toward a well-heeled buyer.

The next Times Mirror regime, under a new publisher, Richard Schlosberg III, hit the ground running with extensive employee morale measures and community activities that showed respect for Denver and its future. Schlosberg headed the United Way and was a key figure in starting the new convention center and the Greater Denver Corporation's drive for cleaner air, metropolitan unity, and a new Denver airport. The *Post* was given a new $56 million printing plant (on land purchased by Guittar) and regained the Sunday circulation lead with an innovative marketing program linked to a successful TV magazine. Furthermore, under editor David Hall, the whole *Post* staff shared in winning the prestigious Pulitzer Prize gold medal for public service on April 17, 1986, the highest national recognition of the *Post*'s overall quality in its history.

However, economic clouds that had been barely visible in the early 1980s, when Times Mirror bought the *Post*, now darkened the whole Denver landscape. Energy firms were going out of business, the Denver real estate market was slipping into chaos

---

of Dallas to revamp the *Post*, so this sketch is biased. But it was a bias shared by at least some in Times Mirror, for Guittar returned to Dallas and was replaced as *Post* publisher by Richard Schlosberg III in July of 1983, and most of the Dallas management crew was gone from the *Post* within the year, and from Times Mirror soon thereafter. They had refashioned the look of the paper, redirected *Empire Magazine* from a western to an urban focus, deployed endless marketing surveys, dissected the Mormon church and the *News*'s former editor in two lengthy series, and won a Pulitzer Prize for photography. But their formula did not succeed in selling Denver on the new morning *Post*, either in circulation numbers or service, or in the affections of the bulk of the newspaper's staff, as revealed by later employee surveys.

(a state of affairs that later became explicit in the city's savings-and-loan scandals), and the retail department store trade shook with the loss of the Denver Dry Goods Company, a principal *Post* advertiser. In addition, Times Mirror was undergoing a national restructuring, shedding acquisitions that were not performing to the standards of Wall Street, which reflected management imperatives in a publicly held communications company during the Reagan years.

Thus *The Denver Post* was sold again to an affiliate of the privately held MediaNews Group, which took control on January 1, 1987, ending the Times Mirror era after six short years. The *Post*'s link to the *Los Angeles Times* was to be expressed not by fraternal publication but by contributing to the California paper its admired young publisher, Schlosberg, who became president of the *Los Angeles Times* and later a senior vice president of Times Mirror. On the bright side—and by this time *Post* employees were used to discovering brighter sides—the new *Post* owners had a very successful newspaper history and were acquiring a much-modernized, slimmed-down, "leaner and meaner" newspaper with skillful staff grimly determined to survive.

IV

On December 1, 1987, *The Denver Post* came under new owners for the second time in the economically turbulent 1980s and for the fifth time in its near-century of publication. Dean Singleton, thirty-six, and Richard B. Scudder, seventy-four, bought the paper for $95 million and burst into the Denver newspaper wars during the worst business recession since the 1930s. In this economic storm, the *Post*, though unbowed, had been bloodied by a weakened advertising market; Times Mirror had reportedly lost almost $9 million in its last full year of operation, an admitted distress to a major public corporation with a short-run eye on Wall Street. By contrast, Singleton and Scudder were confirmed private operators with a longer-run view. In just four years they had formed the non-public MediaNews Group with some fifty-six newspapers, including several "turn-around" challenges but mostly middle-sized, small, and newly profitable properties.

Singleton and Scudder had within the year waded into two other metropolitan challenges, the *Dallas Times Herald* and the *Houston Post,* with energy-bust market problems akin to *The Denver Post*'s. Given the unprecedented speed of their metro acquisitions and their obvious taste for risks, the new bosses, relatively unknown to the beleaguered *Post* staff and to Denver, seemed about as maverick a pair of newspaper gamblers as were Bonfils and Tammen when they bought the *Post* in somewhat similar economic circumstance.

Actually, the Singleton-Scudder team had as much if not more hands-on newspaper publishing experience than any of the other owners who had come to the *Post.* Singleton, a native of Graham, Texas, had been in the business since age fifteen, and was noted for rescuing insecure dailies, with, as Scudder put it, "a rare ability to cut costs without sacrificing quality." Singleton told the *New York Times,* "While your total dedication may be to the news product and to the causes you can fight for, if you don't have a solid profit base, all else is meaningless."

The *Post* staff had absorbed the lesson that profits were desirable as the mid-1980s economic bust worsened, and the truth was also bred in Scudder's bones. His grandfather had founded New Jersey's largest newspaper, the *Newark Evening News,* in 1882, and Scudder had risen from reporter to be its highly successful fourth-generation publisher. He was also widely respected in the newspaper industry for technological innovations such as pioneering the de-inking and recycling of old newsprint. The Garden State Paper Company, which he founded in 1960, is still the world's largest manufacturer of newsprint recycled entirely from used newspapers, a matter of great environmental importance. While most of Scudder's newspapering had been in the East, he had ranched near Edwards, Colorado, and was familiar with the Mountain West and the *Post.* So the newspaper was getting experienced ownership that sought like experience in its chief lieutenants and soon hired as the new *Post* leader Maurice J. "Moe" Hickey, fifty-three, the Gannett Company's publisher of the *Detroit News* who had also helped establish as successful new papers *Today* in Florida and *USA Today* nationally. Hickey began newspaper work as a teenager in Maine and was an aggressive, hands-on commander of every detail of competitive metropolitan publication. His *Post* regime was marked by a mercurial management style reminiscent of Bonfils, with considerable turnover of personnel. But it substantially improved circulation delivery, printing quality, and editorial packaging, and it added a third line of presses to the *Post*'s new plant at Fox Street and I-70, just west of the Valley Highway. This enabled the end of all printing and the awkward distribution of newspapers from the old plant at Fifteenth and California streets, and under Hickey the newspaper could thus efficiently consolidate editorial and business offices at its present Denver Post Tower above Civic Center.

When Hickey's management style wore thin with a *Post* personnel already overchurned by the Times Mirror Corporation, the new owners turned to the more equable but equally experienced Donald F. Hunt, sixty, a longtime Canadian newspaperman who co-founded the *Toronto Sun,* had been publisher of the *Houston Post* from 1983 to 1987, and was a MediaNews international executive. He took over the *Post* on October 27, 1989, and was joined shortly by F. Gilman Spencer, former editor of the *New York Daily News,* as the *Post*'s twelfth top editor.

MediaNews had immediate goals for the *Post* in 1987: achieving financial stability in the face of the deepening local recession, consolidating modern newspaper operations at its new locations, and introducing state-of-the-art computerized and electronic business, editorial, and printing technology. In addition to technological innovation, the Hunt team further streamlined the editorial package, reduced newsprint consumption, pushed quality color printing as good as any in the country, negotiated competitive wage and benefit packages with a staff that loyally recognized the shaky conditions of the market, and put the whole paper on its most stringent financial diet in recent times.

From this base, the news side expanded sports and business coverage, attacked such late 1980s metropolitan stories as the new international airport and the savings and loan scandal, and provided in-depth coverage of such regional stories as the Yellowstone fires, Colorado River depletion, and Hispanic problems along the Rio Grande. The front-page vigor of news display had roots in Spencer's experience of newspaper street wars in New York City, and, in much more sophisticated fashion, of the "news circus" methods of Bonfils and Tammen. The editorial page under Chuck Green won the prestigious Sigma Delta Chi national public service award, and overall the *Post,* though decidedly slimmer, became better organized and printed more colorful sections than ever. Its lifestyle and fashion emphasis hit well with younger readers, along with a retail advertising market slowly reviving with such developments as the new Cherry Creek Shopping Center.

As a result, MediaNews, by the end of 1990, and after investing some $10 million, had *The Denver Post* turning the 1987 operating losses into solid profits, increasing competitive share of the retail and classified advertising market, dominating the national advertising field, and—an almost unheard of feat at least in *Post* history—delivering the paper consistently by 6 A.M. From 1987 to the first quarter of 1991, daily circulation increased from 230,130 to 252,944 and Sunday circulation from 391,693 to 416,558. Thus, *The Denver Post* entered the 1990s with new financial stability despite a still-depressed advertising market. This achievement of 1987 goals for MediaNews was a good signal that the newspaper would charge vigorously into its second century.

V

That aspect of any American newspaper most difficult to explain to the general reader is its split organizational personality, which is the peculiar product of our national communications history. As with most papers, *The Denver Post* is both a private manufacturing business and a public-interest community institution. Sometimes, as this book has tried to suggest, these two roles have not been easily combined in a tempestuous century of widely varying personalities and policies.

As a private business, the durable *Denver Post* has survived by making profits—sometimes large, sometimes slim—from sales to readers and advertisers in an increasingly competitive market. But as a community institution, it has built and maintained editorial credibility only by news coverage and opinion expression that is as objective as can be humanly achieved—which is to say, reasonably insulated from the personal opinions and biases of business, community, government, stockholder, employee, or other interest groups.

This independent editorial role, and its insulation from the newspaper's business concerns, has been greatly strengthened over the *Post*'s century. It has become so strengthened because of the growth of professional editorial ethics within the newspaper industry, of the support of those values by the courts under the First Amendment, and of the recognition by readers that an independent press helps guarantee their own constitutional freedoms in our society.

By the time Frederick Bonfils and Harry Tammen brought the *Post* its first commercial success around 1900, the American press had generally achieved independence from political party or governmental control. But further First Amendment free-press guarantees began to be widely codified only in the 1920s when professional editorial ethics also began to mature. It was hard for buck-hustling business proprietors like Bonfils to realize that newspaper editorial ethics were maturing. Bonfils was both editor and publisher; as editor he was fiercely independent of political parties and business organizations, but his concept of the newspaper was that of a personal fiefdom, answerable only to his own values, which included mixing news and opinion whenever, and of hustling dollars wherever. At that time there was scarcely the body of First Amendment law or thinking in the courts about the newspaper's role in American society that came to be established only a few decades later. By the post–World War II era when the *Post*, under Palmer Hoyt, was making a national name for itself on First Amendment matters, the courts were giving newspapers protection for their public role that would have been unthinkable, and perhaps undeserved, in the era of the "circus" journalists.

The Tenth U.S. Circuit Court of Appeals, turning back complaints from a dissident stockholder, ruled in 1972:

> A corporation publishing a newspaper such as *The Denver Post* certainly has other obligations besides the making of a profit. It has an obligation to the public, that is, the thousands of people who buy the paper, read it, and rely upon its contents. Such a newspaper is endowed with an important public interest. It must adhere to the ethics of the great profession of journalism. The readers are entitled to a high quality of accurate news coverage of local, state, national, and international events. The newspaper management has an obligation to assume leadership, when needed, for the betterment of the area served by the newspaper. Because of these relations with the public, a corporation publishing a great newspaper such as *The Denver Post* is, in effect, a quasi-public institution.

These private-business and quasi-public functions of the *Post* have varied over the century in the vigor and skillfulness with which they have been managed, against the backdrop of a surging and always highly competitive market. In tough economic times, such as the mid-1890s at the start and in the decade of the 1990s, the private business considerations of the newspaper have been forced closer to center stage. Whether it was Bonfils and Tammen putting out their first Sunday edition in 1898—an impressive sixteen pages for some 20,000 readers—or Donald Hunt and F. Gilman Spencer producing a recent issue of some 200 pages for more than 400,000, *Post* managers have ridden economic tigers always more fierce in hard than in easy times. Especially in the tough times of the 1990s, it is always difficult for business and government officials to be comfortable with editorially independent newspapers. When the publishers and owners of a newspaper are deeply involved in community business problems, when everyone is scratching to improve economic conditions, why let editors and reporters cover the negative aspects of things? The champions of civic good, sincerely focused on a cause, cannot really understand that while the *Post* may support their cause in general, it must point out its shortcomings in particular. There is such a thing as the public interest in having full information, and in the full right of dissident expression, even when it involves the Chamber of Commerce.

Two great public works projects along the Front Range come to mind, both of which the *Post* has alternately supported and criticized in various ways. In the Bonfils era, beginning about 1912, the vision of the great railroad-and-water Moffat Tunnel through the Rockies began to take shape. *The Denver Post* castigated the entrepreneurs of the tunnel for their cost estimates and project enthusiasms, yet finally supported legislation favoring the project. Later the newspaper again attacked cost overruns and management frailties but hailed completion of what eventually became a historic boon to the community.

There are obvious parallels between this not-so-long-ago chapter and the *Post*'s relationship to the new Denver International Airport. As a business, the *Post* contributes substantially to the community support of the project, and on its opinion pages it has supported the airport consistently, although giving objectors ample voice. And in the news columns, none could say that the shortcomings and perils of the evolving project have been neglected. But this pro-and-con of airport coverage has at times made little sense and greatly discomforted the more dedicated airport supporters. They do not understand, as with the Moffat Tunnel and endless other community issues over the century, that it is the *Post*'s role to be both a community critic, operating as a public-interest institution, and a community supporter, operating as a major private business. These two roles have been the great internal tug-of-war, push-and-pull factors of *The Denver Post*'s first century, and the tension between them will still be with us in the second, thanks to the entire First Amendment and the Bill of Rights.

Epilogue

These sketches of *The Denver Post*'s colorful first century end as they began, on a note of economic struggle. At the *Post*'s birth in 1892, a bevy of tiny papers scrambled among themselves. In the early 1990s, just two Denver dailies, swollen by 100 years of technological change in the newspaper industry, compete just as vigorously—now as much against new forms of electronic media and changing readership habits as against each other's editorial or business agendas. When Bonfils and Tammen bought the *Post* in 1895, they took advantage of new forms of presses, mechanical typesetters, telegraphic news services, and such young wonders as improved typewriters, telephones, and cameras. These enabled much larger, and much more costly, "mass market" newspapers for the new reader population flooding the growing city. This constant change of newspaper publishing technology into the complex computerized web presses of today is one theme of the *Post* story that a focus on personalities and public issues cannot adequately capture.

This technological growth is partially indicated by a list of the labor unions that have served the *Post* so well over the years, without a major strike or shutdown and with a degree of loyalty to the paper uncommon in many other cities. In 1892 the International Typographical Union and the Denver Stereo typers and Electrotypers Union were both in place. Other unions arrived in the Denver Mailers Union, 1897; the Graphics Communications International Union for engravers in 1901 and for pressmen in 1906; the Circulation Employees Association, 1930; the Denver Newspaper Guild for editorial employees, 1938; the International Association of Machinists, 1948; and the Denver Paper Handlers Union, 1950–51. All of these groups have adapted with great skill to new printing and circulation techniques that could not possibly have been foreseen a century ago. No sketch of this paper, however brief, could overlook these major labor organizations and their interplay with the different ownerships and managements over time—nor the hundreds of other unorganized employees who have made this newspaper a vital engine in the growth of its community and region.

In that city-building process, *The Denver Post*, like other metropolitan dailies, has played a number of roles: it has distributed information in the form of news, advertising, and entertainment features; it has aided government by criticism or policy suggestion; it has helped develop the city or region's economy and culture through business activity, and by philanthropy; and, in the process, it has become a major national political "voice" of the Mountain West. For example, to celebrate its 100th birthday in 1988, the National Geographic Society published a new *Historical Atlas of the United States* in which it mapped the Sunday newspapers that dominated various regions in geographic spread. West of the Mississippi, these were the *Minneapolis Star Tribune*, the *Kansas City Star*, in Texas the *Dallas Morning News* and the *Houston Chronicle*, the *Arizona Republic* of Phoenix, the *San Diego Union*, the *Los Angeles Times*, the *San Francisco Examiner* and *Chronicle*, the *Portland Oregonian*, the *Seattle Times*, and, right in the center of the Mountain West, *The Denver Post*. These papers covered the most counties surrounding their core metropolises, and even in 1982, when these particular statistics were gathered, the sunday *Post* as the "Voice of the Rocky Mountain Empire" was well positioned not only in Colorado but throughout Wyoming, western Nebraska and Kansas, and northern New Mexico.

If changes in technology empowered this regional grasp in the earlier part of the century, they also changed and challenged it by the end. Through new technology, more and more people now get their immediate information about the world from radio, film, and television. And regional newspapers such as the

Post also confront national editions of such papers as the *New York Times, Wall Street Journal,* or *USA Today,* and a host of specialized magazines and special-niche publications. These new elements have reduced the almost total public dependence upon the daily newspaper which was the hallmark of any western community until well after World War II.

But the printed newspaper survives as a unique if embattled civic institution, as is certainly demonstrated by the *Post's* history. As Leo Bogart, an eminent newspaper historian, puts it:

> The ability to read is now an integral part of the civilized human heritage and is destined to remain so. Does that mean that the daily press must inevitably be part of what we read? Why can't we do our reading from computer terminals or use books and periodicals to supplement the top-line information we get from broadcast news? The answer must be that our world is increasingly complex and specialized and human affairs are more interdependent. The constantly changing information on which people depend is simply too voluminous to be replenished at less than daily intervals. The record requires a continual update, which radio and television provide for only a handful of stories at a time. . . . Each day's paper is a distinctive and irreplaceable record of that place and date. It embodies the collective memory without which no society can exist.

In this sweeping technological change, the much-discussed "information revolution" of our time, survival of a metropolitan daily newspaper such as *The Denver Post* has to be considered a major achievement of business management, and of the printed newspaper's necessity to the community. But it is also a function of civic and reader loyalty that can only have been built over time. This development of reader and community loyalty has been the consistent goal of *The Denver Post* over the years, from Bonfils and Tammen to MediaNews.

The remarkable record of *Post*-generated philanthropies is a case in point. Without the contribution of *Denver Post* dollars through the Bonfils and Tammen families, many of our major civic landmarks might not be with us—the University of Colorado School of Medicine, for which Frederick Bonfils gave the land; Children's Hospital, which the Tammens so generously endowed; Holy Ghost Church; the Belle Bonfils Blood Bank; the Denver Center for the Performing Arts; Bonfils Hall at the Museum of Natural History; the Loretto Heights library; and a myriad of other institutions which the Bonfils sisters, Helen and May, helped to take root. And in addition to such ownership gifts made possible by this newspaper's business success, there have been the contributions of the newspaper itself, the thousands of dollars raised for Christmas charities in 1991 being just the latest in a long stream. The point in listing these is not to stroke the *Post*'s reputation, but to illustrate the special bond that any enduring newspaper must have with its community and its readers.

In *The Denver Post*'s case, a century of history has kept this bond strong. One sad example. Just before Elizabeth McCourt Doe Tabor, who was once wed in the presence of the president of the United States to her silver king, was found frozen to death in a mining shack, the confused old siren had anxiously asked if she had been on the front page of *The Denver Post* lately. The *Post* and Baby Doe had bonded, while she was both on her way up and on her way down. And as the "Voice of the Rocky Mountain Empire," *The Denver Post* in its first century has done a good job of bonding with the West through many ups and downs—or so it seems to one participant who has been privileged to be a part of *The Denver Post* for a third of its century.

Index